The Closing of the Net

M ONICA H ORTEN

The right of Monica Horten to be identified as Author of this Work has been asserted in accordance with the UK Copyright, Designs and Patents Act 1988.

First published in 2016 by Polity Press

Polity Press
65 Bridge Street
Cambridge CB2 1UR, UK

Polity Press
350 Main Street
Malden, MA 02148, USA

ISBN-13: 978-1-5095-0688-0
ISBN-13: 978-1-5095-0689-7(pb)

A catalogue record for this book is available from the British Library.

Library of Congress Cataloging-in-Publication Data

Names: Horten, Monica, 1960- author.
Title: The closing of the net / Monica Horten.
Description: Malden, MA : Polity Press, 2016. | Includes bibliographical
  references and index.
Identifiers: LCCN 2015034995| ISBN 9781509506880 (hardback) | ISBN 1509506888
  (hardcover) | ISBN 9781509506897 (paperback)
Subjects: LCSH: Internet--Political aspects. | Internet--Law and legislation.
  | Corporations--Political activity. | Copyright and electronic data
  processing. | Interactive multimedia--Moral and ethical aspects. | BISAC:
  COMPUTERS / Internet / General.
Classification: LCC HM851 .H687 2016 | DDC 303.48/33--dc23 LC record available at
http://lccn.loc.gov/2015034995

Typeset in 10.25 on 13 pt Scala by
Servis Filmsetting Ltd, Stockport, Cheshire
Printed and bound in the UK by CPI Group (UK) Ltd, Croydon

The publisher has used its best endeavours to ensure that the URLs for external websites referred to in this book are correct and active at the time of going to press. However, the publisher has no responsibility for the websites and can make no guarantee that a site will remain live or that the content is or will remain appropriate.

Every effort has been made to trace all copyright holders, but if any have been inadvertently overlooked the publisher will be pleased to include any necessary credits in any subsequent reprint or edition.

For further information on Polity, visit our website: politybooks.com

Contents

Acknowledgements

The aim of this book is to understand how political events could change the way that the Internet functions for the average user. What I'd noticed in my research since 2006 was a series of small political changes that were apparently unconnected to each other but seemed to be pointing at an outcome that would somehow restrict people's ability to use content, services and apps. I wanted to see if I could make sense of this set of unrelated events. I found that when I put them all together and began to unite them into a single volume, the common elements did spring out. If one looked at them from a conventional policy perspective, the sense would not be there because then each event would be in its own little silo of 'net neutrality', 'privacy', 'filtering' and so on. Policymaking tends to stick with these kinds of silos, and identifying the need for action is therefore determined by the technology, and the policy literature very often follows suit. Hence a privacy scholar would rarely meet a copyright scholar or a net-neutrality or media scholar. If you 'do' privacy, you perceive that you have little in common with copyright colleagues.

It was because I crossed those boundaries that I have found many friends, contacts and academic colleagues working in all of the different disciplines, but all have one thing in common, namely a sceptical feeling that something is going in an adverse direction, and many also have a positive desire to protect the open Internet. I have been sent unsolicited papers by academics working in all of these fields. Out of genuine interest I turned up at the Computers, Privacy and Data Protection Conference in Brussels and hung out for an evening with a group of privacy advocates. My long-standing professional work in telecoms meant I was delighted to speak at the European Competitive Telecommunications Association (ECTA) conference and listen to debates on investment in telecoms infrastructure. I went to Broadband World Forum and watched a demonstration of deep-packet inspection, with the same curiosity as I went to the Internet Service Providers Asssociation (ISPA) legal seminar on data retention. I accepted the offer to be on a panel at Centre for European Policy Studies (CEPs) with the head of the French Hadopi, just as I spoke on a quite different panel at Re:publicca in Berlin with La Quadrature du Net. I was privileged to attend a conference on net neutrality in Strasbourg at the Council of Europe, and to address trainee lawyers for the US military in a Washington DC luxury hotel. I sat on the public benches of the Old Bailey listening to *Twentieth Century Fox* v. *BT*, where the drama I'd been writing about played out before me. I've been lucky enough to be a panel speaker at a European Parliament Seminar; and to have launched my first book there.

All in all, I've met many of the people who have a part to play in this book, in particular people in the EU institutions, Members of the European Parliament and the Brussels lobbying community. I've not only met people with whom I agree, I've also met those with whom I disagree, and I feel that this has laid the foundations for a richer understanding of the issues. They come from right across the spectrum of political views: from one of the founders of The Pirate Bay to the Motion Picture Association's European legal counsel; from leading privacy advocates to Facebook's lawyers; from members of the Internet Governance Forum to AT&T's Brussels representatives. All of these people have in some way helped me to understand what is going on in the political sphere.

However, their comments and input would have made no sense without an understanding of the political process. From a theoretical perspective, I am influenced by theories of new institutionalism; however, for this book, I've analysed the case studies using structural power theory. My methodology, developed over several years since 2006, is about linking text to power. Political institutions speak through the written word, set out in documents, sometimes very long and complex texts in which are buried the key nuggets that will create change. I've gathered those documents together and collated them in what is becoming a rather comprehensive personal electronic archive of policy documents. What I've been able to do is to link the nuggets in the text to the external political agendas, and follow the processing of them in the legislatures to try to establish where and what is influencing these very crucial policies that will affect the Internet, and determine whether or not it remains open.

I have quite a few personal thank yous and acknowledgements. I am grateful to the Department of Media and Communications at the London School of Economics for giving me the opportunity to be a Visiting Fellow, and especially Robin Mansell who mentored me, and Nick Couldry who supported me in getting this book published.

I am also grateful to Elen Griffiths and the staff at Polity Press, and Andrea Drugan who had confidence in me when I first presented the proposal.

It has been an amazing experience serving on the Council of Europe's Committee of Experts on cross-border flow of Internet traffic and Internet freedom, and what I have learned there has fed into my thinking for this book.

I would like to acknowledge the kind assistance of Jan Philip Albrecht MEP, as well as Alexander Alvaro, Catherine Trautmann, Baroness Sarah Ludford, Marietje Schaake MEP, and the office of Pilar del Castillo MEP. I am indebted to Joe McNamee of European Digital Rights (EDRi) who has been a continual source of support throughout my research, and who has given me many insights into Brussels policymaking. I am also grateful to Frederik Zuiderveen Borgesius who encouraged me to think about the politics of data protection.

The assistance of the Secretariat and members of ISPA and EuroISPA was indispensable. Many others have provided input to the book in some way, and I would like to acknowledge the help of Erzsébet Fitori, Kirsten Fiedler, Gordon Lennox, Luca Belli, Andres Guadamuz, Innocenzo Genna, Robert Amsterdam, Peter Traung, Christian Wiese Svanberg, Matthijs van Bergen, Javier Ruiz, Erik Josefsson, Pal Zarandy, Michael Rotert, Nigel Hickson, Jean-Jacques Sahel, Miriam Artino, Caroline de Cock, Felix Treguer and Martyn Roetter.

Finally, I'd like to thank my fellow Fellows at the LSE, Melanie Dulong De Rosnay, Didem Ozkul and Jo Pierson, for some great discussions.

Acronyms and Abbreviations

ACLU	American Civil Liberties Union
ACTA	Anti-counterfeiting Trade Agreement
AmCham EU	American Chamber of Commerce in Brussels
AT&T	American Telephone and Telegraph Company (original meaning) now AT&T Corporation
BBC	British Broadcasting Corporation
BPI	British Phonographic Industries
BSkyB	British Sky Broadcasting
BT	British Telecom
CDPA	Copyright, Designs and Patents Act
CEPS	Centre for European Policy Studies
CMBA	Creative and Media Business Alliance
DMCA	Digital Millennium Copyright Act
DRIPA	Data Retention and Investigatory Powers Act
ECHR	European Convention on Human Rights
ECJ	European Court of Justice
ECTA	European Competitive Telecommunications Association
EctHR	European Court of Human Rights
EFF	Electronic Frontier Foundation
EU	European Union
EuroISPA	European Internet Service Providers Association
FAA	FISA Amendment Act
FBI	Federal Bureau of Investigation
FCC	Federal Communications Commission

FISA	Foreign Intelligence Surveillance Act
GCHQ	Government Communications Headquarters
IAB	Internet Advertising Bureau
ICC	International Chamber of Commerce
ICDP	Industry Coalition for Data Protection
ICE	Immigration and Customs Enforcement
IFPI	International Federation of Phonographic Industries
ISP	Internet Service Provider
ISPA	Internet Service Providers Association
MEP	Member of the European Parliament
MPA	Motion Picture Association
MPAA	Motion Picture Association of America
NSA	National Security Agency
PRISM	code-name for an NSA surveillance programme collecting data from content platforms
RIAA	Recording Industry Association of America
SACD	Société des Auteurs et Compositeurs Dramatiques
TTIP	Trans-atlantic Trade and Investment Partnership
USA PATRIOT Act	Uniting and Strengthening America by Providing Appropriate Tools Required to Intercept and Obstruct Terrorism Act

CHAPTER ONE

Power and the Internet

We live in a world where there is a growing concern about corporate power and its role in shaping our lives, but how often do we ask how it is done? The sceptic in us suspects that the way it is done is anti-democratic, especially when we see a law that seems to relate to a known corporate agenda, but the nature of corporate influence frequently remains behind closed doors. We also live in a world where the Internet has become the dominant means of communication. More than 3 billion people worldwide have Internet subscriptions.[1] They prefer email or instant messaging over traditional phone; they use online videophone services; they like social media over old media. Although we are led to believe a narrative that the Internet is empowering, and we may even see it as 'ours', there is a significant level of corporate interest that can control what we do and is able to wield political power. The way that corporate power might shape the Internet will therefore have a significant effect on the lives of the billions of people who use it. Do we ever think about who it is that has that control, how it might be applied and even how it might be fought over between corporations?

This book is about the big corporations with an interest in the Internet and how they shape political agendas. The main concern is that these corporate interests may conflict with the public interest and the outcome could be that the open Internet becomes restricted or closed. These big global Internet and telecoms firms have the power to shape access to knowledge via their control of a global information infrastructure. Anyone with the power to shape knowledge has the power to shape the way people think. They have another power too, and that is the power to threaten or preserve the privacy of individuals.[2] These two powers together pose a series of complex political questions as to how states should deal with these corporations whose business models are based around the control of data flows. These firms are driven by commercial imperatives and, whilst their intentions are not necessarily malign, the outcome could be one that is negative for individuals. It's not only a matter of how companies may use or abuse these powers, but also how the demands of other interests influence such use. Those other interests could be rival industries, such as film and movie companies, or they could be states. If these powers are left unfettered, corporations and states would be free to take actions that violate fundamental freedoms such as free speech and privacy rights, and to do so with impugnity. Citizens' fundamental rights should not play second fiddle to the interests of big business, and policymakers should understand the risks entailed when drafting policy.

In this book, how these firms exert political influence will be explored through different scenarios related to recent political agendas concerning the Internet. These scenarios address deep and divisive controversies such as net neutrality, network filtering, data-profiling, communications traffic data and copyright enforcement. The kinds of tactics companies use to influence public policy are examined, and we uncover the possible outcomes for the Internet and for citizens' rights.

The power to shape access to knowledge can be understood by taking some very simple examples. A little scene that I observed recently on a train journey seemed to me to encapsulate it. Next to me was a young couple, both students aged about twenty, and evidently in love. He sat facing her, leaning forward, his hand on her knee and looking upwards at her face in a traditional lover's pose. You would expect me to say next that they were staring romantically into each other's eyes – but they weren't. They were staring with intense concentration at two separate smartphone screens. His was a Samsung;

hers was an iPhone. He was thumbing down his Facebook page in total silence, checking a mixed thread of sports news and videos. She tapped messages to friends on WhatsApp. The contrast between the classical lovers' pose and the intense draw of new technology could not have been more striking. For me, the scene created a stark image that exemplified the changing ways in which people obtain news and information. There are many similar scenes played out on trains and in public places every day, all over the world. Smartphones, with more than 2 billion of them in use worldwide,[3] are replacing the newspaper, the magazine, the television, the cinema, the letter or the phone call. Today, what people read, know and understand is all governed by what comes via their screens, and that is why the power of the companies that control access to those screens becomes critically important.

Consider, too, the narrowness of the prism by which information is now viewed. The 5 × 3 inch (14 × 7.2 cm) screen is smaller than an average old-fashioned postcard, yet it is the window on vast amounts of information that people are trying to view, analyse and ingest. No longer do people see a spread of articles before them, able to lightly dip in and out with just a quick glance – now they scroll through a moving thread of headlines ranging from BBC Sport to a friend's amateur video, all viewed in a matter of seconds, and in a narrow, vertical frame.

The companies who deliver content have their targets within a fingertap of desire. This is a paraphrase of the old Coca-Cola maxim 'an arms' reach of desire', coined by its former chairman Robert W. Woodruff,[4] who used it to articulate the idea that power lies in distribution and in infrastructure. Mr Woodruff developed the marketing strategy that Coca-Cola should be available for sale in large numbers of small outlets and vending machines, so that it was as near as possible to the customer when they felt thirsty. It is widely recognized that Mr Woodruff's strategy led to Coca-Cola's international dominance over rival soft-drink companies. Going back to the Internet, the fingertap of desire means that content is readily available on everyone's personal smartphone or computer, to quench their intellectual thirst for information – and all they have to do is tap their finger. Think again about that young couple on the train and how casually they were searching and accessing content, and consider how much power might be held by the person or company that controls the system that transmits such content. And consider it in the context that Facebook's stock-market valuation is higher than Coca-Cola's.[5]

The fingertap of desire creates tremendous possibilities for Internet corporations to have control over so very many aspects of our lives. They can shape the way we visually see content on our screens. Equally, they can shape what is transmitted to us. Shaping what is transmitted means they can block or allow, drop or forward, pick and choose or give preference to content. We are witnessing the creation of a new industrial elite that has power on a global scale, able to control what we are allowed to know, with additional powers to exclude.

This view of the Internet is at odds with the commonly held and widely advocated empowerment narrative that the Internet is open and free, encouraging innovation, free trade and democratic speech. How can the Internet be at once empowering for the individual, and at the same time controlled? The dichotomy between the ideal of the open Internet and the possibilities for industrial control[6] has created a combative political environment that will be explored in this book by examining the political activities of the Internet companies, and the rival interests that want them to take action.

Structural power and the Internet

The power to shape access to knowledge implies what is known as 'structural power', a term first coined by the scholar Susan Strange in 1988, in her book *States and Markets*.

Strange defined the term as the power to shape and determine the structures of the global political economy within which other states, their political institutions and their economic enterprises have to operate.[7] Structural power is distinct from economic power. Where economic power is exercised by mobilizing capital and controlling markets, structural power involves creating outcomes that determine the opportunities and limitations for the society at large. In other words, it's not about goods and prices, but about what society and individuals can do. It is frequently exercised by influencing policy and lawmaking and shaping political agendas – in other words, lobbying is an important component. And with an analysis that has proved to be remarkably prescient, Strange had observed that changes in technology had swung the balance of factors over which states have control.[8] In particular, she suggested that structural power may be exercised across international borders by multinational corporations and is not constrained to individual countries or jurisdictions.[9]

The easiest way to understand structural power is to think about infrastructure – the equipment and processes that run essential functions for society. Industries that hold structural power have the ability to facilitate things that the state wants to do, or to obstruct them, and they make choices that determine what we can or cannot do. They make the arrangements for systems, and therefore can create systemic changes. For example, the banking system and its institutional structures determines the availability of credit, so changes in that system will have effects rolling right down to individuals. The large retailers control the infrastructural arrangements for the supply of food. They make choices at national or global level that determine the prices of groceries for consumers, and changes in their systems will determine what we can eat. The power companies that run the electricity grid have the ability to determine the availability of essential functions such as cooking and heating homes. Inherent in all of these examples are changes that will shape the choices available to policymakers.

For example, if a change to power-supply arrangements creates disruption to the electricity grid, it means that people cannot heat their homes. That is why governments regulate the electricity companies in order to ensure a continued supply.

Susan Strange identified four primary structures of power: knowledge, security, production and finance. The four factors all relate to essential functions in a democratic society. We will focus here on the first two – knowledge and security. Knowledge is relevant because that is the primary function of the Internet. Security is relevant because the data gathered from the knowledge function may be used for surveillance purposes.

Knowledge structures control the way that information, science and culture are recorded and disseminated. The power of knowledge structures lies in their ability to determine the means by which knowledge is transmitted, how it may be stored and retrieved and who communicates it.[10] Think of the business maxim 'information is power'. This is also true in a wider sense of society. The organization which develops the channels for the dissemination of knowledge is controlling the means of access – transmission, storage and retrieval – for something which is of value to all of society, even though its economic value may be intangible. The power in the knowledge structure is most easily maintained by limiting access, and that is a way for those who control it to defend their position, especially where they hold a monopoly position. Because they have control of transmission, storage and retrieval, controllers of the knowledge structure are also able to deny access to knowledge. States often find this power useful, and seek to harness it to maintain their own control of knowledge through censorship. This may be political censorship, or it may have a social goal to protect society from 'bad' things, or it can take the more benign form of a licensing system. Denial of access[11] is therefore a key notion when we consider structural power and the Internet, and several cases of restriction or denial of access to content are discussed throughout the book.

Traditional knowledge structures relate to the distribution of books, music and film. They comprise retail outlets and cinemas.[12] Knowledge structures also relate to the international telephone system and other electronic communications such as data networks. Today the Internet has taken over from those traditional knowledge structures and is the dominant one, combining all of those functions – books, films, music, telephone, messaging – in one global networked system. The Internet is now deemed to be an essential service for society, with more than 3 billion users worldwide,[13] and it runs across borders. The corporations that run the Internet make the arrangements that determine how we can communicate and how we access or distribute information. Importantly, they can either give or deny access to information. Hence the infrastructure that comprises the Internet is a source of structural power and states have a great interest in building relationships with the organizations which run the infrastructure.

The Internet infrastructure is designed so that we, the users, can find content – where content means films, books, pictures, blogs, news, information videos, games and shopping sites – without needing to know where it is. It can be on any computer, anywhere in the world. We just need to know a single address, and the content will be brought to us. The system takes a user's request and passes it on, then, having retrieved the content, the system brings it back to the user. That individual content request will travel via a range of different technologies, over cables, WiFi, satellite or mobile phone. For example, a laptop could be connected via WiFi, which then goes via a modem over the phone wires and then on to a trans-oceanic cable, before finding the content and returning to the user with it.

In fact, the Internet infrastructure is rather like an iceberg. The content that we see is like the part of the iceberg that floats on the ocean, but below the waterline are layers and layers of technology that make the whole thing possible. The key to understanding the structural power entailed in the Internet, is to understand those layers below the waterline. The layers have a critical function in separating the operation of the physical network from the content, which sits on top of the whole structure. The physical network, or layer, is at the bottom and comprises the wires and cables, transmitters and signalling equipment. At the top are the application and presentation layers.[14] The World Wide Web, which enables access to content and services, is found here. In between is the IP layer,[15] containing the routing mechanisms that organize and transmit data. In the IP layer, the data is divided into little packets that consist of a header (the source and destination addresses) and the payload (the data of interest to applications). The header is inspected by routers on the network, which forward the packet as appropriate. This forwarding action will be repeated many times until the packet reaches its destination where the data will be put back together again in the right order and forwarded upward through the layers for display on the user's screen.

The Internet, as a network of networks, is quite different from anything that had previously existed. The layered design was intended to minimize the power held by the network providers because the content was on the top of the network and not integrated in it. Anyone operating the physical links did not have to be concerned by the applications or content. Similarly, anyone using an application did not need to worry about how the data would be physically transmitted. The network was designed to ensure the end-to-end transmission of the data, without interference and without the sender or recipient needing to modify what they were doing. This is also known as the end-to-end principle[16] and it was a fundamental principle of the Internet architecture. It was critical in the growth of the Internet into the global network that it is today because it meant that anyone could attach an application or build one, without having to obtain permission. It all operated using standard, open protocols, meaning that multiple networks could be connected together in such a way that a built-in resilience was established: data transmission would continue even if one of the physical links broke. Transmitting in packets (technically known as packet switching) enabled greater efficiency, increasing the amount of data that could be carried on any given link, and data travelled from one end to the other without interference. All the intelligence – that is, the equipment that determined how information should be displayed, transmitted and routed – was at the edges of the network, whilst the network itself remained a 'dumb pipe'.

The Internet was a general-purpose network[17] open to all. Access to content was provided by the World Wide Web, a universal application that worked on any hardware or software, meaning that content could be set up by anyone and all users connected to the network could reach it. The Internet is therefore often referred to as an open network. Its open character led to an explosion in innovation and in content, which in turn is why the openness is considered to be worth protecting as something that has an intrinsic public-interest value.

The expression 'net neutrality'[18] is frequently used in this context. It is sometimes used to encapsulate the notion of the 'dumb pipe' and the open character of the Internet that provides a platform for innovation where players have equal terms of access. It was coined by the legal scholar Tim Wu, who articulated it as a non-discrimination principle, enshrining negative interference with traffic on the network.[19] A more vivid way to describe this negative interference principle is 'no blocking, no throttling, no paid prioritization'.[20] However, 'net neutrality' has become a loaded term in the political context, and one over which every Internet expert has a view. My preferred definition is one drafted by the Dynamic Coalition on Network Neutrality of the Internet Governance Forum, and it is that 'net neutrality is the principle that all traffic is treated without discrimination, restriction or interference regardless of its sender, recipient, type or content'.[21]

The reason why there is a political issue surrounding net neutrality is due to interference within that layered structure of the network that affects – or denies access to – the content that the user can view. The middle layers of the network can be programmed to interfere with traffic flows. Depending on where and how it is done, such interference may mean that people cannot use certain applications at certain times. Network providers will 'shape' traffic in order to deal with congestion at busy times, but, if permitted, they could also do it for commercial purposes. The middle layers can be programmed to monitor content access and they have the capability to intercept, view or collect data on every single webpage that an individual visits. They can block or filter content across entire websites or domains, or just on a single page. The same technology can be used to develop 'personalized' services, so that each individual user gets a different kind of service. Hence, the network providers control the access to the Internet from people's computers, smartphones, tablets and other devices, and they control the links between the user and the content. They control the arrangements for granting or denying access to knowledge and do so for billions of fixed and mobile subscribers, and so they become determinants of people's behaviour online. This is the knowledge dimension of structural power at the network level.

Above the network is the content, linked via the World Wide Web, and a parallel knowledge structure subsists in the large content platforms, which are web-based services that offer the opportunity for users to upload their own content via a standardized means of presentation. The information they host includes images, video games and so on that are uploaded by users. In general, they are the social media sites, blogging sites, image and video upload sites: Facebook, YouTube, Instagram, Twitter and Google sites, for example. Their standardized presentation offers the opportunity to publish, but also restricts the way that it may be done, hence they shape the way in which knowledge may be formatted, displayed and retrieved. Some limit the format of content even right down to the number of characters transmitted. To take a few examples, Twitter limits messages to 140 characters; Facebook imposes a timeline format; Instagram is a photo gallery; Yelp has a directory format. Search engines help users locate content wherever it is on the Internet, and hence shape the way in which knowledge may be located, and they are essential components of a content platform. It is especially true for search engines because through their algorithms they determine what we find in any given search. The content platforms also have monitoring and blocking abilities, as well as the ability to track users' behaviour and profile their viewing habits. The tracked behaviour is used to enable the 'free' provision of services, and may be used to limit the user's access to content according to his or her own preferences, creating a kind of 'filter bubble'.[22]

The content platform providers exercise structural power by establishing processes and formats that dictate the terms on which we may format the information that we upload or transmit. A select few content platforms have become particularly powerful, with huge multinational operations and supporting infrastructure – typically data-processing centres – in more than one country. In 2015, Facebook accounted for around 1.3 billion of the estimated 1.7–2 billion social media users globally.[23] Twitter was estimated to have 200–300 million monthly active users, and Google's social media platform Google+ had a similar number.[24] Some sources have suggested that 1.6 billion social media users access their accounts from a mobile phone.[25] These numbers give an idea of the economic power of the content platforms, but, to illustrate further, one needs to look at how it is being leveraged by others. Take this example: at music festivals, fans wave their phones in the air, taking photos of themselves and the musicians. The practice is so prevalent that some 1.5 million photographs were uploaded to Instagram during the three-day Glastonbury music festival in 2014.[26] Festival producers now try to work social media uploads into their marketing mix because of the high level of customer testimonials that it provides for them. It's an example of how a technological development has facilitated a change in social norms, created a commercial opportunity and reinforced the structural power of the content platforms.[27]

Ultimately, it is a combination of the network providers and the content platforms that drives the fingertap of desire. The postcard-size screen implies that the content will have to be adapted for the user to make sense of it. The sources of information on the networks are vast, but the funnel to the end-user is narrow. This structure enshrines tremendous power to shape the choices offered and narrow them to fit the funnel. It makes the providers very powerful indeed because they can control the means by which knowledge is discovered, and on what terms it may be communicated.

The security structure

The other primary structure of power that is relevant in the Internet context is security. In the context that Susan Strange would have conceived it, this was about the protection against violent conflict.[28] In other words, it was about military security. Governments and people seek protection from such conflict, and are often prepared to pay a high price for it. So they may sacrifice or restrict other liberties in order to save lives. They sometimes grant privileges to those in a position to offer security against loss of life. The person who can provide such protection frequently gets into a position to exercise political power, because they have the ability to determine or limit the choices available to society.

In the context of this book, security is more about counteracting threats. There are many non-violent hazards that occur in civil society where people value security, such as the threat of financial fraud. Similarly, security is valued regarding the threat of Internet viruses, attacks by hackers, fraudulent or malicious emails. Security on the Internet generally seeks to ensure that the traffic on the networks flows smoothly without disruption and to remove these types of hazards for the general benefit of all users.

Security may also be about one's private life and correspondence; for example, if individuals are put under threat for their beliefs. In this book, security is interpreted, in line with human rights thinking, as the protection of individual privacy, where intrusion on private lives and correspondence presents the threat. The networks and content platforms act as guardians of our privacy, but may also be requested to divulge private information to the state or other commercial companies. They have the ability to threaten or protect the security of individuals and of the state, and this is the essence of their power.

The security structure is therefore about the data of individual communications, including emails, chat, gaming, social media and web-browsing. This personal data is gathered for every communication and every webpage request that anyone sends, anywhere in the world. It is collected by both network operators and content platforms, and, importantly, it forms the basis of the business revenues of the content platforms. This has opened up opportunities for Internet companies to build new business models, based on data. They know from the data where people shopped and what they bought, and even where they were standing or sitting when doing the transaction. That data is sold to advertisers, who use it to target prospective customers. The names of those clicking a 'like' button for a particular brand are sold to commercial competitors of the brand, who will use the data for targeted advertising. The data is mined and processed to create profiles of individuals in order to offer them products and services that are closely matched to their perceived needs. This is known as behavioural targeting. The profiles, too, are bought and sold, hence they have a commercial value for the companies.[29] This explains why advertisements on screen are frequently similar to something that has been previously viewed. It's also why social media profiles may appear on a website that the user has previously had no relationship with.

In these ways, personal data underpins the business model that enables the services to be provided for free, precisely because it can be traded. It means that users get 'free' use of a wide range of services[30] such as search, photo albums, daily diary, keeping in touch with friends and the ability to post opinions to the world. With some 2 billion users of content platforms worldwide, and more than 1 billion of them on Facebook,[31] it is not surprising that some policymakers believe data is the new 'oil' of the world economy. It is certainly true that the content platforms have become some of the largest and most powerful corporations in the global market and their revenues are increasingly being chased by the network providers, who are adopting similar data-driven business models. Data-profiling creates a form of structural power in shaping access to knowledge because of its ability to shape the delivery of content to the user, and by limiting the preferences of the user it can also deny access to the content because the user simply never knows it is there. As the studies in this book will show, this power can be used to advantage.

The reason that data-profiling forms part of the security structure is because of the potential intrusion on privacy, and so it has become a political issue. The data that is collected is not just that which is voluntarily put online by users, but it also includes data gathered by monitoring and tracking, and data that has been inferred from the monitored behaviour. For example, the system has the ability to monitor online friends and link that data back to a real name, in order to infer an attribute such as ethnicity or sexuality. Location data enables a user's activities to be tied together in time and space.[32] Someone who was not openly gay could be inferred as such, based on his online friends and places visited, and he could be classified for commercial or political purposes. This kind of classification can drive advertising that is intrusive or causes embarrassment, but there is also a risk that it could be used to underpin discriminatory practices. There is a further risk that it drives excessive personalization of the services offered to that user, leading to a kind of 'filter bubble' which has the effect of limiting that user's access to information and even shaping their thoughts.[33]

It is chilling to feel that someone is watching as you read, shop or browse. Contrary to the empowerment narrative, a Belgian academic study has found that individuals have little control over how they are tracked.[34] They don't know what is being used, how or by whom. They would also feel wary if they thought they could be put under suspicion for what they are interested in, or that their data was being passed on to third parties without their permission. When people do learn that they are being monitored, they tend to self-censor. Hence there is a risk that the avaricious data-gathering, monitoring and targeting of individuals and their personal preferences could begin to limit the richness and empowering possibilities of the open Internet.

Privacy is a fundamental right and states are duty-bound, under international human rights law, to guarantee the privacy of their citizens. This includes the right to a private life and the right to private correspondence. There is case law to show that correspondence means emails, phone calls and Internet usage.[35] However, it's also true that most people will do things for convenience without pondering the price they might pay for it.[36] Could it be that we have accepted a kind of Faustian pact where giving up our data is the price of 'free' services? Some critics suggest that this notion of the Faustian pact is trite and extreme. Other experts say that, on the contrary, the Faustian element is much more sinister than I have portrayed it, pointing out that Facebook and its subsidiaries not only have our socio-economic data and life patterns, but also our location data, messaging data and potentially our purchasing and credit data.

The political difficulty is compounded because all of that personal data collected by content platforms or network providers is of interest to governments themselves. People who are willing to enter into a pact with industry, in return for something that improves their lives, are not so willing to do it so that governments can snoop. Industry then finds itself conflicted between the trust of its customers and helping the government. It's arguable that this conflict of interest gives them political leverage to negotiate other bargains with governments. Governments have conflicting policy choices in seeking both to placate industry and meet their duty to guarantee individual rights and freedoms. In the European Union, that duty is enshrined in the Treaties that incorporate the European Convention on Human Rights (Council of Europe 1950), as well as the more recently agreed Charter of Fundamental Rights.

Shaping policy

The combined might of the knowledge and security structures presents a risk that a new type of content gatekeeper will emerge. The effect could be that they would prevent publication or control availability or selectively promote information. This is what is meant by the notion of 'closing the net'. It would no longer be an open network equally available to everyone. The bleakest vision is that the closed Internet could become no more than a glorified interactive television. However, the more likely outcome is not a definitive vision of blackness, but rather fifty shades of grey – there will be gradual closing up of the opportunities to upload and publish, as well as to download or access content. From a political perspective, this is a more problematic outcome. Selective blocking or filtering is about censorship, whether it is imposed for commercial purposes such as enforcing copyright, for social goals or for political purposes. Selective, preferential delivery of content via personalization and data-profiling techniques can have a similar effect to censorship by limiting the options to the user[37] and not informing the user that there is a wider choice out there. There is a very real risk to free speech, but if it happens in an ad hoc way, as is likely, it will be more difficult to see where and how the censorship or preferential selection is happening, and hence also more difficult to deal with it.

Those who own the infrastructure have the ability to determine how things should be. They control the arrangements. Their objective is to defend their control over the infrastructure and to prevent any (from their perspective) unwanted erosion of their power. They do not want to be told how they should operate their systems by the state. In other words, they do not want regulation. They do want the maximum freedom[38] to grow their business. Indeed, as we have already said, the ownership of the infrastructure is the source of their power. If the state tries to regulate the way they operate, they fear a loss of power.

Therefore, the Internet corporations seek to shape law and policy in order to defend their structural power. It's also true that the state wants to maintain a good relationship with them because of their economic size and the critical importance of the services they deliver to the functioning of society. It is a kind of symbiosis between the state and the corporations. The corporations need the state (which may be a national government or a supra-nation entity such as the European Union) to guarantee the conditions under which they can carry out their business. They may also ask the state to remove obstacles to doing business. The state needs the corporations for moral and financial support. The modern state institutions have grown side by side with the big corporations since the Industrial Revolution,[39] and, in that light, this is just a continuation of a historical trend[40] of the large telecoms corporations working with government. Corporations wield influence due to long-term conditioning of government institutions, and it's worth remembering that several of the telecoms companies have roots going back to the nineteenth century.

Policymakers have tended to encourage a 'light touch' regulation of the Internet industries, preferring self-regulation to a regime imposed by law. This has stemmed from a belief in the market-led benefits of the Internet,[41] a belief that justified policies to drive privately funded infrastructure development. The dominant vision or construct in most policymakers' minds concerned positive network externalities such as faster production of goods and lower transaction costs, supporting broader policy aims of growth and prosperity.[42] The idea of information as a commodity,[43] and the possibility of perfect control over transactions that the Internet offered, appeared rational and logical, and therefore had a certain appeal. Hence, the monetization of personal data was viewed as a benefit in the new economy. The metrics for policy success became aligned to those of the markets without any concept of the negative externalities.

The policymaking perspective contrasts starkly with the empowerment narrative, where users feel that the Internet is 'theirs' and not that of the corporations. This attitude derived from the early Internet which was promoted by some of its proponents as a place free from governments and corporations,[44] and those early users enjoyed its non-establishment culture. The Internet was inspiring for innovators, and empowering for users. The Internet was set up with its own governance system, which its founders believed would keep out governments. It was a system of private administration and global governance bodies that would manage the evolution of the core technologies, as well as the underlying network. The Internet had been deliberately set free of the regulatory system that governed the telecommunications industry. In the EU, Internet access services were classified as 'Information Society services', granting them immunity as 'mere conduits',[45] and providers were freed from regulatory obligations to provide universal service, as well as from other transparency, pricing or audit obligations.[46] Users bought the message of empowerment that was used to encourage people to go online, and in their eyes the Internet was about freedom, not constraints.[47]

The empowerment narrative is supported by human rights advocates, who argue in favour of the open Internet as a necessary corollary for free speech in the twenty-first century. The Internet is the means by which individuals exercise their democratic rights,[48] and where they go for ideas, information and knowledge.[49] The European Court of Human Rights has established that the right to freedom of expression is fully applicable to the Internet,[50] and it is a two-way right[51] to both access and publish ideas and information without interference from a public authority. There is case law to suggest that blocking and filtering of Internet content potentially violate the right to freedom of expression because those actions constitute interference.[52]

There is therefore a sharp political divide between the user-empowerment narrative and the market-led perspective of policymaking. Whenever laws are proposed to address Internet issues, the sticking point is generally found in the clause or element that encapsulates the difference between these two perspectives. Policymakers do not want to be seen as restricting free-speech rights, but they struggle to create the necessary political compromises with industry.

Nowhere is this divided narrative more sharply established than with the issue of copyright enforcement. This is an especially contentious agenda, led by the entertainment industries, challenging the structural power of the Internet industries. The entertainment industries, primarily music and film, sought to restrict access to content that allegedly infringed their copyrights. The structure of the Internet has radically altered the value proposition for the large entertainment and content companies. In essence, it removed their control over the distribution of content. They readily blamed the ease with which their content could be copied, but this is too simplistic an explanation. The digital media enabled a new freedom to circulate material that had previously been locked up either in physical product formats or in heavily regulated broadcasting agreements. This explosion rocked the underlying value chain structure. Where the entertainment industries had established business relationships with the bricks-and-mortar intermediaries – cinema chains, book and record stores, video rental outlets and television broadcasters – they found that in the Internet ecosystem, their content was being distributed through new start-up companies with whom they had no business relationship, and who – in some cases – did not want a business relationship with them. Deals based on copyright contracts were blown apart, hence copyright enforcement became a major issue in the Internet space. This is an inter-industry battle that has been pursued over many years. In this book several instances are highlighted where the entertainment industries have used political leverage to target the structural power of the Internet industries, demanding that they take action against alleged copyright infringement. The structural power and political influence of the large Internet and entertainment corporations, together with the ramifications for Internet restrictions, are uncovered by the cases in this book. The data-driven knowledge structures of the content platforms, and the implications for their political power, are discussed in chapter 2, with reference to how they proactively defend their business model at a political level in a battle over a new privacy law in Europe. Chapter 3 delves deeper into this theme, to see how the US authorities supported their industries in the EU political arena, and in doing so also supported the requirements of their intelligence services. The requirement for communications traffic data and its structural power ramifications are addressed in chapter 4. The power of the large telecommunications corporations is discussed in chapter 5, in the context of the political agenda for net neutrality. This theme is continued in chapter 6, which looks at the specific context of content-filtering, and how Internet service providers (ISPs) who are asked to filter without a proper legal basis may respond by pressuring states to avoid net neutrality policies. Chapter 7 considers how corporations who want stronger copyright protection tried political tactics to manoeuvre the structural power of the Internet service providers via 'cooperation' on the policing of content. This role of the Internet industries in policing content continues in chapter 8, which considers more ways in which the entertainment industries and other interests sought leverage over the structural power of the large content platforms and of the ISPs. The underlying thought in chapter 9 concerns cloud computing services, which are the emerging new structures of the Internet, and how a heavy-handed attempt to shut down one such service, Megaupload, could send a signal to other structural innovators.

This brings me finally to the reason for writing this book. I was identifying connections between the different political agendas of privacy, net neutrality and copyright. The cases inform us about the ways in which the political decision-making is interconnected and therefore also about how the outcomes of apparently isolated policy initiatives will impact on each other. Privacy policy closes off certain possibilities for copyright enforcement. A social goal to filter content may alter a government's position on net neutrality. Demands for copyright blocking orders leads the way for other interests to do the same. Decisions on data-profiling send ripples through the entire infrastructure. Data is a source of power in itself that may underpin other political bargains. The cases suggest that there is unlikely to be a one-directional march to a closed Internet, but they do indicate where and how restrictive practices will happen. They help us to identify the interests – which organizations want it, and why they want it. Most of all, such cases signal that an understanding of these political agendas is critical in order to see who controls that fingertap of desire and what is truly at stake for the future of the Internet.

CHAPTER TWO

Private Lives, Public Policy

There is a very fine line between protecting privacy and the game of politics. At stake is whether privacy law protects our private life or whether it determines how industry may process our data. Is the law protecting the liability of industry or is it protecting us? Whilst we perceive a 'data-protection law' should protect our private life and information about us, in fact, policymakers are establishing political compromises that facilitate industrial uses of our data. Publicly, politicians may profess to protect our data, but in truth their actions often belie their statements. Their job is actually to get a piece of legislation adopted by parliaments. In order to get the necessary majority when the legislation is voted, they need to ensure that they obtain the agreement of different political parties. Although it must be balanced against the need to protect fundamental rights – and privacy is a fundamental right[1] – states tend to believe that the market should lead policy[2] and these kinds of political agreement may serve a variety of industry interests.

This chapter is about the political influence of corporations that gain structural power from the processing of personal data, and specifically it relates to those who trade in personal data within their terms of service. Power in the knowledge structure comes from consent, rather than coercion,[3] and when we look at the large content platforms such as Facebook, Google, Twitter, Instagram and so on, with a combined active user base in 2015 of 1.7 billion,[4] that concept gains a special meaning. This is an industry that has only existed for some fifteen years but is now a global business worth billions of dollars. They offer services that are apparently 'free', but the price is that the users give up their data, with the risk that they also lose their privacy. 'Free' services equate to continual surveillance, creating a modern form of the Faustian pact[5] that is very much a reality in the online world. The political issues concern what they are allowed to do with our data and how far they may intrude, and the notion of 'consent' has become a source of political tension.

In order to put this into context we'll turn back to 1990, when Europe was taking its first step towards data-protection law to protect privacy. There was a heavyweight lobbying campaign to temper the proposals in favour of what the industry wanted. The proposed new data-protection directive aimed to harmonize the regulatory regime for the processing of personal data across all EU member states, incorporating a principle that individuals should be able to control the use of their data. It's important to remember that, in 1990, the Internet was not yet available to the public and the data-processing industry was in relative infancy. Processing of data mostly concerned business-to-business transactions, and the exchange of information between companies that were starting to trade electronically. Examples cited by the International Chamber of Commerce (ICC) in 1992[6] were transfer of personnel files, travel information, credit records and so on. In that context, business organizations like the ICC began to advocate on the importance of exchange of information for international trade, and the need to protect trans-border data flows. Given that context, three elements of the European proposal annoyed the industry lobbyists. These were restrictions on the transfer of personal data to third countries; a requirement for express consent for use of personal data; and an obligation to notify the supervisory authorities.

The International Chamber of Commerce (ICC) said that any requirement for the users' express consent would be an 'administrative burden' because individuals would be confronted with repeated requests for consent and it would increase the cost of service provision. The ICC further argued that restrictions on trans-border data flows would pose all kinds of problems, including difficulties in operating cash-machine networks, hampering computer backups and electronic ordering of goods, as well as causing problems for the processing of personnel and health records, and it accused the EU of 'hampering innovation' and 'placing undue burdens on companies'.[7] However, when the directive was eventually adopted in 1995,[8] it did require the unambiguous consent of the individual and the incorporation of restriction on transfer to third countries.[9] This restriction created problems for US companies trading in Europe because they did transfer data back to the US, and an agreement was brokered with the US government, known as the 'safe harbor' agreement, which had consequences that rumbled on for years (see next chapter).

By 2001, the Internet was a dynamic and growing system, and was becoming a force for advertising. For example, figures from the UK's Internet Advertising Bureau proudly claimed that Internet advertising was worth £154 million per year, equal to 1 per cent of all advertising expenditure and trebling in size every year. The conduct of online advertising was just starting to get on the political agenda when the European Union proposed a new e-privacy directive to deal specifically with data-privacy issues on electronic networks, including the Internet. The matter of using cookies to monitor people's behaviour on websites and use that data for advertising purposes became a political issue. In drafting the proposal, the European Commission had taken the market-led view that requiring consent for cookies would inhibit European competitiveness. However, the European Parliament believed it was necessary to protect the privacy of Internet users. The Parliament inserted amendments to address cookies, and in particular to ban their use without the prior consent of the user. This provoked an industry-led 'save our cookies' campaign from lobbying organizations such as the Internet Advertising Bureau.[10] In the Council of Ministers, the member states were also split between the British, who wanted to protect industry, and the Germans, who already had a tougher national law and were concerned not to compromise it. The final outcome was a political compromise that allowed all parties to move forward; notably, it provided for a cookie opt-out: websites would be expected to inform users about their cookie usage and give them the opportunity to reject cookies. This was acceptable to the nascent online advertising industry.[11]

By 2012, the Internet had grown exponentially and so had the online advertising business. Looking back at that 2001 figure of £154 million per year, the growth is quite astonishing. By 2012, in Britain alone, online advertising was worth £5.4 billion.[12] Growth was fuelled by mobile and social media advertising, where mobile had come to be worth £526 million (up from just £29 million in 2008). By 2014, online advertising in Britain was worth £7.1 billion or around 40 per cent of total advertising spend, and growing at £1 billion per year; social media advertising was worth £922 million, or 23 per cent of the total. Across all of Europe the total value of the online advertising market was more than €24.6 billion.[13] No wonder the IAB said that 'the Future looks bright with consumers spending more time connected', and it is not surprising that they would try to defend their business. It was said that data was the new oil, and as such it should be allowed to flow unhindered. Personal data has become a highly valuable asset. The market for analysis of large sets of data is growing by 40 per cent each year worldwide. The currency of this new digital economy is data and, in many cases, personal data.[14]

Alongside the economic power, the structural power of these businesses had also grown. The large content platforms and social media sites controlled the way that knowledge and ideas were disseminated and they were responsible for shaping the way that content was displayed on the screen, whether fixed or mobile. The search engines determined how information could be found. Between them, these companies controlled that fingertap of desire.

The year 2012 was the one in which the review of the 1995 directive was due. A new European law was proposed, known as the Data Protection Regulation. The regulation was the responsibility of the Justice Commissioner, who headed the section of the European Commission that looks after fundamental rights. The institutional positioning was crucial because it set the political positioning of the regulation as a privacy-protection law and it highlighted the divide with industry, which wanted economic objectives to take precedence. The regulation had set out to deal with new issues that had arisen since 2001. An underlying concern, from the privacy perspective, was that of behavioural targeting. This is a form of advertising that tracks people's online activity and the data collected is used in order to present advertisements to the consumer.[15] Their web-browsing habits, location, social media, search terms and even email conversations may be tracked in order to build up digital profiles of their interests and purchases. All kinds of information, such as gender, age, ethnicity, and shopping and browsing preferences, may be collected in order to create profiles of individuals. Behavioural targeting therefore entailed the observation and bulk processing of billions of people's behaviour and it was the factor that enabled users to get the 'free' services. Hence, it drove the lobbying effort of the content platforms.

In some cases, the profiles could be pseudonymous – that is, individual but nameless[16] – where any personal identifiers, such as names and email addresses, would be stripped out and replaced with a numeric code or tag. The issue was whether or not a pseudonymous profile was personal data. Academic experts, as well as European data-protection authorities, argued that it was, because the tagging could lead to the identification of individuals.[17] Industry lobbyists questioned that view, arguing that an individual would not be personally identified.[18]

This division of opinion is why the matter of consent became a political issue. Since 2009, European law has required consent to be given for the placement of tracking cookies on a user's computer.[19] Even if they are asked, consumers will frequently tick a box in order to get the short-term gratification of whatever they are being offered, without realizing that the surveillance of their activities is ongoing.[20] However, there was a division of opinion over what action would mean that the user had given consent. The industry lobbyists argued that pseudonymized data should not require 'consent'. Academics and privacy experts argued that it did, and that the consent requirement should be strengthened to ensure that it had been given in a way that was meaningful for the user. Thus, 'consent' formed one of the central political arguments over the Data Protection Regulation.

Transfer of data outside the EU was the other point of contention. The content-platform industry, with data centres outside the EU and especially in the US, did not want restrictions on where they could process data. Nor did they want to be told to respect EU regulation when moving data internationally. Hence, they advocated for a relaxation of rules on transferring data to other countries,[21] in order to reflect the international structure of their data-processing operations. On the other hand, the industry did want a more unified set of data-protection regulation across Europe, so that it would be the same in each country, because having to deal with twenty-seven different sets of regulation was proving expensive.[22] The Justice Commissioner, Viviane Reding, released the draft regulation[23] on 25 January 2012.

It proposed putting controls on the type of processing that could take place (where 'processing' means how they use and manipulate it). It also imposed restrictions on data transferred out of the EU into other jurisdictions, and regulation of 'pseudonymized' data. All of this was enforced by steep fines for non-compliance. Unsurprisingly, the industry lobbyists did not like many of these provisions. In particular, there was a requirement for explicit consent for data-processing, as explained in Recital 29. There was also a proposed fine of up to 2 per cent of turnover for non-compliance.[24] What was strange was that a provision safeguarding international data transfers, requested by non-EU courts, had been removed (Article 42 – see next chapter).

A long and heated lobbying campaign followed, with the aim of getting the proposal amended along the industry lines. The core of the lobbying came from some fifty or so different organizations and firms. Many of them were lobbying coalitions. These coalitions were significant because they served to amplify corporate voices. They provided a political megaphone, endowing the industry agenda with an apparently wider acceptance because, for example, they could claim that a larger number of jobs were at stake, which makes it more appealing to politicians, who like to think they are acting for a majority interest.

The lobbying activity began immediately after the release of the Commission's proposal. A coalition calling itself TechAmerica expressed its concern about the 'damaging impact' of the proposed new rules. Data-protection policies, according to TechAmerica, should not 'unnecessarily inhibit technological innovation and global information flows',[25] nor should they 'make it difficult for global businesses to operate and invest in Europe due to greater legal uncertainty, increased administrative burdens and the risk of fines'.[26]

When one considers that TechAmerica represented some 1,200 US technology firms – and incorporated the former Information Technology Association of America, an alliance of 350 tech firms including Amazon, eBay, AT&T, Verizon and Microsoft – then its opposition to the pro-privacy proposals is in line with what we would have expected from them. Its position was echoed by another group calling itself Digital Europe, which claimed to represent '10,000 companies employing two million citizens and generating €1 trillion in revenues'.[27] Its members were European and American technology and telecoms companies, including Research in

Motion (BlackBerry), Alcatel-Lucent, Nokia-Siemens, Huawei and Cisco (network equipment); and Apple, Motorola and Sony (mobile phones), as well as the powerful content platform Google. In line with the industry position, Digital Europe advocated that 'the requirements for consent should not be set artificially high, such as requiring explicit consent in all cases'.[28] It is not clear how much influence Google had on the Digital Europe position, but it is reasonable to assume that this coalition offered it another route into the European institutions in addition to its own direct lobbying.

In other words, here were the large and powerful technology corporations banding together to lobby against the elements in the law that did not suit them. TechAmerica's threat to withhold investment was one that European policymakers had to take seriously, as in this quote from one of its lobbying documents: 'This is particularly troublesome at a time of an unprecedented crisis when Europe needed to attract investment, business and growth.'[29]

The political sensitivity surrounding data protection caused the Commission's proposal to be delayed by a year. European policymaking brings in all three institutions, and it is the role of the Council of Ministers to set the political priorities every six months. But the Council had been reluctant to move forward. In January 2012, the Danish presidency ignored the regulation, as did the Cypriot presidency which followed in the second half of 2012, so the new regulation was not properly established on the policy agenda until the Irish presidency in 2013 – an interesting move because Facebook's European headquarters is in Ireland.

That meant the European Parliament could start work on it in earnest. The rapporteur, Jan Philipp Albrecht, was a German Green MEP. It is unusual for a Green MEP to be given the rapporteurship of an important and large piece of law such as the Data Protection Regulation. The Greens are a small group in the European Parliament and lack the power that is accorded to the larger Socialists or the majority

European People's Party (a conservative group). Mr Albrecht, a lawyer who projected a relaxed image, was highly regarded among colleagues. Many observers were convinced that he was the man to make strong changes in favour of privacy protection, although most of them knew the difficulties that he would ultimately face.

However, Mr Albrecht's appointment[30] prompted a mobilization of industry lobbyists. In fear that Mr Albrecht would promote a pro-privacy law, potentially even stronger than the Commission's proposal, they began a campaign against him. Mr Albrecht gave a harrowing description of his experience:

> They tried everything to weaken my position [. . .] At the beginning they lobbied me. Then they realized that lobbying others might be more efficient. They went to the Council. They tried to prevent me from being rapporteur. They tried to find weaknesses to de-legitimate me. Then they tried to be best friends and came to talk to me to change my mind. And then they sent people to simply waste my time.[31]

As anticipated, the industry lobbyists did not like Mr Albrecht's report.[32] He issued it on 16 January 2013, and industry lobbyists began publicly attacking it:

> We regret, however, that after months of consultation, the draft report published by the rapporteur, Jan Philipp Albrecht, MEP, missed an opportunity to reconcile effective privacy safeguards with rules protecting the conduct of business – both fundamental rights under the EU Charter.
> Going forward, we urge members of the European Parliament, starting with the LIBE Committee, to take into account the important contributions emanating from other committees, and to enact legislation that maintains user trust while encouraging innovation and entrepreneurship in Europe. Achieving this result will require a thorough examination of the proposal and should not be rushed.[33]

The most powerful stakeholders came out against Mr Albrecht's report. The Digital Europe coalition, with Google as a member, did not like around a third of Mr

Albrecht's proposed changes to the Commission's draft text. It proposed a total of 110 amendments, complaining of 'useless paper trails' and 'unnecessary costs'[34] that the draft law would create. Facebook submitted two amendments that vindicated the notion of the Faustian pact, because they sought to make 'consent to the processing a condition of access to a service which may not be otherwise free'.[35] On the subject of profiling, Facebook was adamant that the regulation did not allow content platforms sufficient scope for service customization, and failed to draw the right balance between 'protecting individual rights and safeguarding innovation and commerce'.[36] The proposal to impose fines as a percentage of turnover for non-compliance was attacked, with amendments tabled seeking to mitigate the circumstances in which they could be applied.[37]

Within a month or so of the publication of Mr Albrecht's report, there appeared a massive volume of lobbying letters and briefing papers. The volume of amendments – around 3,000 in total – was especially remarkable. A majority of the amendments came from industry lobbyists, who handed the text to MEPs in anticipation that they would then table the text.[38] A few dozen amendments also came from the privacy advocates European Digital Rights and Bits of Freedom. It took one and a half years for Mr Albrecht and his team to work through the amendments. There were almost 100 meetings with the other party groups to negotiate political compromises on the more controversial proposals.[39]

By now, Mr Albrecht was facing a well-organized and structured lobbying machine, led by US-based corporate interests, and fuelled by the major content platforms. The lobbying coalitions had all came together in one grand coalition of technology-industry lobbying groups. This was the Industry Coalition for Data Protection (ICDP),[40] and its members were Digital Europe, TechAmerica and others, including AmCham EU, and Edima (Google, Yahoo!, Amazon, eBay, Facebook, Apple and Microsoft), as well as the aforementioned Internet Advertising Bureau (IAB). The ICDP was a significant move.

It gave the firms with the strongest interests in data-protection law, such as Google, Facebook and Microsoft, another way to lever influence. It gave them multifarious ways of ensuring that their position could be put to the European Commission and Parliament in addition to their own direct lobbying. The ICDP had held their launch event in November 2011 at the offices of AmCham EU in Brussels, with special guest, Justice Commissioner Viviane Reding. The event gave them a private audience with the Commissioner, to remind her directly of their priority 'flexibility for innovation' – in other words, insisting that the Commission did not impose new regulations on data processing.[41] Their media release suggested that they had been preparing for this launch since May 2011.[42]

Another lobbying hub for US corporations was the American Chamber of Commerce in Brussels (known as AmCham EU), whose committee on the Digital Economy was chaired by the American telecommunications giant, AT&T. Perhaps it was not surprising that AmCham EU accused the European Union of 'demonizing the technology rather than aiming to limit the existing or potential negative uses of this technology whilst protecting beneficial uses' and begged the EU not to go for a 'one-size-fits-all approach'.[43] Brussels lobbyists working on the Data Protection Regulation told how AmCham EU coordinated a Europe-wide campaign in capital cities of all EU member states. The rapporteur, Jan Albrecht, commented drily in an interview with the author that the German government had been a particular target. In his opinion, the rationale was that if Germany blocked a law, it would not happen and therefore the Internet industries would have wanted to court Berlin officials and parliamentarians: 'if you have a huge IT company and you don't want a law, you'd go to Berlin because it's the most powerful. There is a perception that you cannot out-vote Germany.'

The US corporations also turned to the authorities in Washington. Approaches were made to the US Trade Representative and the Trade Policy Staff Committee regarding the issue of international data flows, led by a business group calling itself the Coalition for Privacy and Free Trade. Appealing to the economic mindset, they highlighted the high stakes for the Internet industries in maintaining cross-border data flows – this being a form of lobbying code for the act of ensuring that data could continue to be transferred from users in the EU to data centres in the US. They called on the US authorities to protect the 'vital relationship between digital trade, cross-border personal data flows, and economic growth',[44] and highlighted what they asserted were the holes in the EU legal framework. There was also a Washington-based 'think tank' called the Future of Privacy Forum, which, despite the name, appeared to be allied to an industry position seeking to weaken the consent requirements. The success of these attempts to mobilize the Washington authorities became obvious in light of the situation described in chapter 3.

At stake here was the industry's ability to bulk-process profiles of individuals for the purposes of profiling and behavioural advertising without the rigorous requirement to obtain consent. AmCham EU, for example, argued that the regulation as amended by Mr Albrecht's report would prohibit profiling 'irrespective of the objectives pursued showing no recognition of the many positive uses'.[45]

The political tension built up around the matter of 'consent' as the legal basis for processing personal data. Under the law as it stood, consent had to be informed, freely given, unambiguous and specific, but it could be either explicit or implied. The draft Albrecht report contained a provision for 'explicit consent'.[46] It was supported by privacy advocates. And, unsurprisingly, it was opposed by the industry lobbyists. Digital Europe argued that it was an artificially high legal requirement[47] and would be difficult, if not impossible, to implement in practice. Moreover, Digital Europe said it would result in new business models being abandoned. The industry argued for what they termed 'free and informed' consent, which would give them more leeway, but then again, that is precisely why the citizen advocates wanted a tighter consent regime. Privacy advocates such as Bits of Freedom and European Digital Rights (EDRi) argued that individuals should be asked for explicit consent, and were especially concerned about the processing of pseudonymized data. The Dutch privacy advocates, Bits of Freedom, had drafted an amendment using the term 'singled out' to address pseudonymization.[48] That amendment was rebutted by the industry lobbies.[49]

Another point of tension concerned the 'legitimate interests' of the companies processing the data. This was a get-out clause for industry – a sort of legal umbrella for them to shelter under. It meant that if they could justify the processing of data as a legitimate business interest, then they could do it, and hence the clause was ambiguous. Mr Albrecht clarified where a legitimate interest might apply and added a new provision for the rights of the individual to override the legitimate interest of the business under certain circumstances.[50] The industry lobbyists objected. Digital Europe said that 'legitimate interest' provision was 'crucial', and the Future of Privacy Forum complained that Mr Albrecht's clauses would 'eviscerate the ability' of industry to rely on the legitimate interest as the legal basis of processing.[51]

Through 2013, the lobbying coalitions began to advocate what they called a 'risk-based approach'. Broadly speaking, they wanted a new get-out clause, such that the content provider or website provider could determine for themselves how much of a risk there was in the data they were processing, and therefore the nature of the consent that would be needed.[52] However, the most politically contentious issue was the transfer of data outside the EU. This issue rose right to the top of the political hierarchy on both sides of the Atlantic. Policymakers in the European Union firmly believed that their framework was superior to that of the United States. They were steadfast in the belief that because the United States did not have a federal law regulating the processing of personal data, the legal protection available to European citizens' personal data was inadequate. Justice Commissioner Viviane Reding was sceptical that US law was capable of providing EU-level protection for personal data. Hence, she believed that transfers of personal data from the EU to the US should be controlled. Meanwhile, the US authorities were being lobbied to press the EU for weaker regulation of data transfers, as here in testimony to the United States International Trade Commission: 'those mechanisms are costly and burdensome and, some say, an unnecessary drag on digital commerce that could be alleviated by the recognition of the US framework as "adequate" by the European Union'.[53]

This brief sketch of the political arguments and the lobbying operation gives an indication of the amount of pressure on Mr Albrecht. However, his role as rapporteur was to find the political balance within the Parliament. It is consistent with the role to set up an appropriate negotiating position and be open to political deal-making.[54] Mr Albrecht's report was eventually adopted by the European Parliament with an overwhelming majority in its First Reading on 12 March 2014.[55] Justice Commissioner Reding was also in agreement and, with two out of the three EU institutions behind him, this reflected a considerable amount of confidence in his report. However, it satisfied neither the privacy advocacy groups[56] nor the Internet industry.[57]

The Albrecht First Reading Report incorporated the risk-based approach advocated by industry. This was a compromise. It permitted industry to carry on with processing pseudonymized personal data for behavioural targeting.[58] Profiling[59] was permitted where the Internet user would have the right to object. Consent had to be 'informed' – not 'explicit'. There was an opt-in for profiling, but an opt-out for online behavioural targeting. Industry would only be permitted to keep the minimum data necessary for their purpose,[60] and they had to protect the data under EU law. Businesses would be seriously proscribed from taking personal data out of the EU.[61] As regards international data transfer, Article 43a – a compromise amendment, the so-called anti-FISA clause, inserted by Mr Albrecht – meant that no court judgment of a third country requiring disclosure of data shall be recognized and companies seeking to fulfil such orders would have to notify the local data-protection authorities and seek approval.[62] Importantly, there was a very tough sanction – up to 5 per cent of turnover[63] – for any breach of those rules. In essence, it was a carrot and stick to the industry. The report was positioned as a 'strong signal for Europe'.

The Albrecht Report can therefore be understood as a political compromise. It was clear that he had given way on some points in order to obtain the agreement of all party groups and, as a result, it did not include the strongest privacy measures that had been expected of it. On the other hand, it did take a stand on the issue of transferring data to third countries, which privacy experts regarded as positive. In fact had events not intervened, Mr Albrecht might have achieved much less. Insiders contacted around one year before had predicted that he could have been pushed towards industry-friendly compromises that he could not agree to, or that he would get no agreement at all. As often happens in politics, events did intervene, in the form of a total outsider – Edward Snowden.

The series of revelations in the media in 2013 by Edward Snowden, a former computing contractor to the US National Security Agency, changed the course of the politics surrounding the Data Protection Regulation. Mr Snowden put into the public domain documents that indicated wide-ranging surveillance of the Internet on a global scale. The sheer numbers – billions of records being collected and searched – were an eye-opener for EU policymakers, as they were for the general population. Whereas, pre-Snowden, it would have been easy to obtain a majority in the European Parliament for an industry-friendly, light-touch data-protection regulation, that was not the case post-Snowden. Even the conservative EPP group was in favour of some tougher measures. National politics played

into the mix too. In Germany, the revelations about mass surveillance caused uproar, since many Germans still remember
the Nazi regime of the Second World War, or the communist
Stasi secret police of the former East Germany. Consequently,
even German EPP members were in favour of a tougher
stance on international data transfers, and they called for the
termination of the politically sensitive 'safe harbor' agreement
(see next chapter).

According to Mr Albrecht, interviewed by the author in
June 2014, the revelation of mass surveillance by the US and
other intelligence services had affected public perception and
emphasized the need for strong data protection: 'it helped
us to say we were on the right track, so let's do it,' he said.
He explained how he led the political discussions inside the
European Parliament:

> The EPP willingness was there from the beginning . . . to
> have protection above the level of the 1995 directive. [. . .]
> The EPP and Socialist groups were wanting to conclude in
> slightly contrary directions, so I had to bring them together.
> We had a general agreement already in July 2013; however,
> the matter of data transfer to third party States was still out-
> standing.[64]

On the compromises he said: 'I think there should be no compromises on consent, but we had to do a compromise.' Even
so, he believed that what he got was the highest existing standard for data protection anywhere in the world.

It would have been optimistic to say that it would end there.
The Council of Ministers watered down the compromise
further towards the industry position. At the time of going
to press, trilogue negotiations between the three EU institutions had begun.[65] And that is how the politics of privacy, with
all of its complexities, became boiled down to a compromise
negotiation in the side rooms of the political institutions. The
sceptical view suggests a realpolitik where the compromise
ultimately had to show some deference to the industry agenda.
This is structural power in action, and it illustrates how the

large content platforms can mobilize the industrial support of the world's most influential technology corporations and the US government, with the result that they not only shape political agendas but they also succeed in obtaining laws that shape even the most private parts of our lives.

CHAPTER THREE

The PRISM Agenda

In December 2012, the US Ambassador to the European Union, William Kennard, gave a speech at a conference on privacy and data protection. He was speaking at a Brussels lobbying conference organized by political events company Forum Europe. Key EU policymakers had been invited, including the European Parliament's data-protection rapporteur Jan Philipp Albrecht, and the European Justice Commissioner, Viviane Reding. Mr Kennard began by saying that 'the United States has great interest in the effort under way to update and reform the EU's data protection rules. The outcome of this process can have profound implications for consumer confidence and economic growth in the transatlantic market, as well as on international regulatory and law enforcement cooperation.'[1] He went on to say that data services formed an essential part of the transatlantic economy and he pleaded for the EU to work with the US on privacy rules as a key element within transatlantic trade policy. Finally, he called for the removal of the proposed restrictions on international transfer of the personal data of European citizens, claiming that the US treated the privacy of all people – Americans and non-Americans – equally.

It was that same Mr Kennard who was later called upon[2] by the EU to answer the questions raised by Edward Snowden's allegations of mass surveillance, exemplified by PRISM, the code name for a programme of data collection from content platforms. Notably, the claim regarding the equal treatment of the privacy of non-US citizens was torn apart, and the motive for the US authorities' intervention in Brussels politics became abundantly clear.

Mr Kennard's intervention, defending the interests of his country's industrial corporations, was arguably all part of his job. After all, when states and corporations have a common interest, they work together to protect it. Moreover, it was the latest in a long line of industry-supporting US interventions in EU data-protection politics. Going back to the early 1990s, when the EU and the US both began developing data-protection law, there had been a divergence in their political approach. The US consulted almost exclusively with corporate interests and, allegedly, its policy was based on a paper drafted by the telecommunications industry. By contrast, the EU consulted data-protection authorities in the member states.[3] As a result, the EU law was premised on protecting individual privacy, whereas US law came from the position of protecting industry interests. In 1990, when the EU drafted its first data-protection proposal, it was concerned to protect its citizens' data against transfer to third countries where it did not receive the same level of protection. In the same year, the US government intervened and a meeting took place between EU and US officials, followed by further discussions in 1991.[4] After the EU adopted the Data Protection Directive[5] in 1995, US industry mobilized and pressured their government because the directive created legal difficulties for them in transferring EU citizens' personal data to the US. Given the volume of trade that required data-processing, this was a significant issue. Moreover, in 1995, the Internet was just starting to emerge as a vehicle for commercial trade and the US technology industry in Silicon Valley had an interest in ensuring they could transfer data. There were several years of negotiation, between 1997 and 2000, in which a diplomatic compromise between the EU and the US was brokered in order to facilitate the lawful transfer of EU citizens' personal data to the US.[6] This diplomatic pact was known as the 'safe harbor' agreement. It means that companies can transfer data between the two jurisdictions without fear of violating EU law, provided that they adhere to certain rules, and they have to register with the US Department of Commerce, which oversees the system. It is described by some as a 'hybrid' of self-regulation and government enforcement.[7] This 'safe harbor' agreement became a long-term weak point of sensitivity in EU–US relations.

In December 2012, when Mr Kennard gave this speech, the Brussels lobbying community was keenly awaiting the release of a report from the European Parliament. It was almost a year since the European Commission's draft data protection proposal had been presented to the Parliament on 25 January 2012; the rapporteur, Jan Philipp Albrecht, had been appointed on 12 April 2012, but his report was not released until 16 January 2013. So anything that Mr Kennard said in this speech was in anticipation of Mr Albrecht's report. The 'safe harbor' agreement was therefore one of the priorities he underscored, calling it 'a valuable element in enabling thousands of American companies to do business in Europe'. He argued that 'there is a need to confirm' that companies and regulators in the EU can continue to share data with 'enforcement agencies elsewhere'.

With hindsight, the speech is very revealing. Although dressed up in diplomatic language, his statements underscored how the US authorities were opposed to the EU position. Mr Kennard deftly combined his government's own interests in surveillance with his country's industrial interests and hinted at those elements that the US might not approve. He gave the impression that he was on the side of industry, and only a very well-informed observer would have noticed how his defence of data acquisition by law-enforcement authorities gave away another agenda:

> For law enforcement acquisition of electronic communications, the stringent U.S. statutes protecting the privacy of email and voice communications, among the highest standards in the world, apply equally to foreign nationals and U.S. citizens. The United States does not discriminate with

regard to judicial redress to obtain access to personal data
collected for criminal investigations and provides opportunities for any person, regardless of citizenship, to correct such
data if it is believed to be inaccurate.[8]

At the time of that speech, the extent of US government
surveillance was still unknown. Subsequently, of course, the
US position with regard to protection of non-US personal
data has proved to be somewhat different from the ambassador's positive picture. The global external surveillance
revealed by Edward Snowden[9] was wide-reaching in terms of
the technologies intercepted and types of data collected. It did
not appear to be governed by stringent rules, and it did discriminate between foreign nationals and American citizens.
It has become evident that the Fourth Amendment rights
enjoyed by US citizens are not guaranteed for non-US citizens, nor for people residing outside the US.[10] This was the
legal basis on which the National Security Agency (NSA) justified its 'external' surveillance of non-Americans. It was this
legal position that drove the issue to the top of the European
political agenda.

Edward Snowden's revelations, which emerged in the
Guardian on 5 June 2013,[11] threw the ambassador's comments into sharp relief. The reason why the US ambassador
would have made a plea for cooperation on data-protection
policy was not just to protect his country's industry, but to protect his government's intelligence services. The ambassador's
unstated aim was the removal of a provision regulating access
by non-EU governments to EU citizens' personal data. This
was the provision (Article 42) that prohibited third countries
such as the US from gaining access to the personal data in
the EU where required by a court order, unless it had prior
approval from EU data-protection authorities.[12] In that context, it can be seen how the underlying interests of the US
for surveillance caused its interests to align with those of its
industry. In defending the industry's interests to transfer
data to international processing centres, the ambassador was

clearly defending the US government's ability to obtain data for mass surveillance. There is no suggestion that the US corporations agreed with the agenda of mass spying by the state, but it is suggested that supporting an industrial requirement for data collection and processing also helped the state to protect its surveillance interests.

NSA surveillance and non-US citizens

The data collected by the NSA came from all types of electronic communications. It included communications metadata, as well as real-time collection of Internet traffic itself. Millions of telephone-call records, including location data, were being requested on a daily, ongoing basis.[13] Bulk email metadata records were being systematically trawled, including the to, from, cc and bcc fields in individual emails,[14] and 5 billion mobile-phone location records per day were being gathered.[15] Hundreds of millions of email address books from users of webmail and instant-messaging services were harvested.[16] The fibre-optic cables carrying the Internet were allegedly being intercepted and traffic siphoned off.[17] It came as a shock to many people that data was allegedly collected from trusted consumer brands such as Google and Yahoo, Skype services, YouTube videos and social media sites such as Facebook – this was the PRISM programme. Under PRISM, emails, videos, photos, voice calls, file transfers and social media were obtained via so-called 'backdoors' to the servers. The companies denied giving direct access to the authorities but did admit that they complied with lawful requests. The existence of PRISM was confirmed by the US authorities, who said it had been operational for six years.[18] PRISM allegedly involved data being hived off on to special servers to which the intelligence services had direct access. In order to make sense of it all, a 'big data' search-and-analysis capability had been developed, code-named X-Key-Score, which allegedly was capable of trawling through media buddy lists, friends and posts, as well as webmail data, IP addresses and webpages visited.[19] The NSA's 'customers' for the output included other US government departments such as the Department of Commerce and the Department of Justice.[20]

Democratic oversight appeared to have been light-touch. Senator Diane Feinstein, chair of the Senate Intelligence Committee, said that Congress had been briefed about the metadata collection programme, although some senators, notably Senator Ron Wyden, had been raising questions about it for several years and were unhappy with the responses they received.[21] The legal basis for the NSA to conduct electronic surveillance on communications networks was established by a law passed by the US Congress in 1978, called the Foreign Intelligence Surveillance Act (FISA). FISA came on the back of a Senate Committee report in 1976. This was the report of the Select Committee to study 'Government Operations with Respect to Intelligence Activities', headed by Senator Frank Church and hence known as the Church Committee.[22] This report found that lawful intelligence collection is vital to the national interest, but interestingly, in light of the Snowden revelations, it warned specifically against the dangers of excessive electronic surveillance. In particular, the Church Committee warned against the absence of checks and balances, and – of specific interest from the European, geopolitical perspective – it included a recommendation that the NSA should only monitor non-American communications. Hence, FISA applied to surveillance of non-Americans only. In their public defence of it, the US authorities repeatedly asserted that such surveillance could not be used to target any US citizen.[23]

This point was central to the controversy. In the US, the concern related mainly to whether data was being gathered from US citizens. In the EU and the rest of world, the outrage was sparked due to the surveillance of non-US citizens. There was a difference in the legal basis for surveillance of people inside and outside the US. Inside the US, a warrant had to be issued and the government had to show probable cause that the target was an agent of a foreign state, whereas outside the US no warrant was required, nor was it necessary to show probable cause.[24] It is suggested in an official report for the White House that the original 1978 Act was a carefully crafted balance between giving maximum flexibility to the NSA and providing safeguards for (American) citizens.[25] If we accept that view, then it seems that the balance had swung way out of kilter by 2014.

Originally, FISA applied only to electronic surveillance – in other words, interception and monitoring on the networks. The law established the FISA court, which authorized NSA electronic surveillance requests. Political oversight of the FISA process was carried out by the Intelligence Committees and the Judiciary Committees of the US Congress.[26] In 1998, FISA was extended to apply to phone bills and call records, and other business records (under what is known in US law as pen register and trap-and-trace orders), with the safeguard that it only allowed the production of a narrow set of these records.[27]

The key rule-change occurred in 2001 after the 9/11 attacks, in a counter-terrorism law called the PATRIOT Act, which amended FISA and allowed the US government to compel the production of communications metadata from the telecoms providers. Section 215 broadened the 1998 provision on the production of records, such that 'records' became defined as 'any tangible thing', and the safeguards against misuse by the authorities were considerably weakened.[28] This was the legal change that opened the door for the mass data collection revealed by Edward Snowden.

According to allegations made in court depositions by the Electronic Frontier Foundation, the NSA commenced an electronic surveillance programme soon after the PATRIOT Act was passed. This programme involved the interception of telephone and Internet communications of US citizens as well as non-Americans, and it was allegedly carried out without a warrant or judicial review.[29] The EFF alleged that the programme was ordered by President George Bush in 2001, and subsequently re-authorized. The allegations were never confirmed.

In 2008, there was a further change to FISA via the FISA Amendments Act (FAA). The crucial element provided for in the FAA was Section 702, a set of procedures for surveillance of citizens of foreign countries outside the US.[30] Under Section 702, there was no requirement to show 'probable cause' or to obtain an individual warrant, and this, according to some experts, would expose the personal data of European citizens to US government surveillance without warrant or proper judicial safeguards.[31] A further provision in Section 702 constrained the technology companies from revealing their involvement in NSA surveillance programmes and gave the network providers immunity for cooperating with the NSA,[32] the effect being to mandate secrecy. It arguably paved the way for the PRISM programme as well.

A report conducted subsequently for President Obama concluded that the FAA Section 702 had been helpful in preventing terrorist attacks, but the question remained whether it had achieved that goal by unnecessarily violating individual privacy.[33] It is alleged that the FISA court rubber-stamped all of the NSA requests,[34] although a FISA court order released in the context of a transparency lawsuit, brought by American Civil Liberties Union (ACLU) and the Electronic Frontier Foundation (EFF), showed that at least one of the judges was concerned about the over-broad nature of the orders sought.[35] A US government report acknowledges that, in 2006, the FISA court took a broad interpretation of Section 215 to authorize the collection of call records and metadata for foreign and domestic calls from the telecoms companies for a period of ninety days.[36]

In this context, it is interesting to see the comment of President Bush's former Defense Secretary, Donald Rumsfeld, in a 2013 interview with the German news magazine *Der Spiegel*:[37] 'My impression is there are a lot of people, Republicans and Democrats in the US, as well as people overseas, who are concerned about the NSA programs. Should people be concerned about their privacy? You bet.'

The nexus of EU–US politics

Viewed from the EU perspective, the NSA's apparently blanket surveillance of EU citizens ignited some very sensitive passions. There evidently were no legal safeguards or protections for EU citizens, but there was liability protection for the telecoms and technology corporations that cooperated. Europeans felt there was a clear ethical dimension – 'partners do not spy on each other' was the response of EU Justice Commissioner, Viviane Reding, who wrote to the US Attorney General, Eric Holder, stating that programmes such as PRISM could have adverse consequences for the fundamental rights of European citizens.[38] Mrs Reding said that the scope of the PATRIOT Act could lead to European companies being asked to transfer data to the US in breach of European law. She underlined a demand for judicial remedies to be available for European citizens, and for US law-enforcement access to European citizens' data to be strictly limited and subject to judicial review. She asked for more information from the US authorities. Hence, a future trade agreement between the EU and US could have been threatened because of the scale of US spying on EU citizens.

The German MEP Manfred Weber, vice chairman of the European People's Party (EPP), the centre-right grouping in the European Parliament, said that 'The mutual trust between the EU and the US has been undermined.' The EPP is usually supportive of business and pro-American, and in this respect Mr Weber's comments stood out. Mr Weber called for a termination of the 'safe harbor' agreement.[39] 'US firms must play the game according to our rules,' he told *Der Spiegel*.[40]

The German Chancellor Angela Merkel and the French President François Hollande both said the NSA activities were unacceptable.[41] The anger of the German public was reflected

by the opposition parties, who accused Mrs Merkel's government of failing to protect Internet users.[42] In October 2013,
it was alleged by the German media that the NSA had been
listening in to Mrs Merkel's mobile phone. This caused a
national scandal, and was dubbed 'Handygate' (the Germans
use the term 'Handy', pronounced 'hendy', for a mobile
phone). Mrs Merkel's reported reaction was that 'we need to
be able to trust our allies and partners. That trust must now
be rebuilt,' but she did not enlarge on how she envisaged that
rebuilding process. In a phone call with US President Obama
she asked for an explanation.[43]

However, it was becoming obvious that Germany had been
kept in the dark. There was a sense in which Germany felt that
the US was treating it as a second-rate partner. An explanation
for this lay in the historic links on surveillance cooperation
between the US and the UK. These links go back to just after
the Second World War, and the UK–US Communications
Intelligence Agreement (UK–USA Agreement) of 1956,
under which the two governments agreed to 'exchange collection of traffic, acquisition of communications documents, and
traffic analysis'.[44] Australia, New Zealand and Canada joined
the collaboration under the so-called 'Five Eyes' agreement,
which remains the basis of intelligence exchange between
these countries today. Germany, of course, was not party to
these agreements because it had only just been liberated from
the Nazi regime at the end of the Second World War in 1945,
and trust had yet to be established.

What further angered the Germans was the allegation,
in German news reports, that the British intelligence services were intercepting a transatlantic fibre-optic cable that
carried German Internet communications.[45] Mrs Merkel's
spokesman told the *Guardian*, 'we are no longer in the cold
war [. . .] Bugging friends is unacceptable.'[46] In an attempt
to quell the public disquiet over the allegation of NSA and
British surveillance of German Internet traffic, the heads of
the Bundesnachrichtendienst (federal intelligence services)

demanded a 'no spy' agreement. However, their apparently tough stance did not satisfy the German citizens. Instead it sparked more political controversy. The German media questioned why a 'no spy' agreement was needed, unless the US had been previously conducting espionage on German territory,[47] to which the government had no answer. It had been felt that a 'no spy' agreement would help to address the public outrage. In fact, they did not obtain the deal they wanted from their US counterparts.[48] The outcome was a written assurance that the NSA and GCHQ would abide by German law and a 'German package' agreeing to provide the Bundesnachrichtendienst with higher-quality information.[49]

In light of that situation, it did seem odd that Mrs Merkel quickly went silent on the surveillance issue, right after the news that her personal phone had been tapped. In October 2013, at a meeting of the EU heads of government, she notably stood behind David Cameron and failed to veto a suggestion to delay the Data Protection Regulation (see chapter 2) until 2015.[50] Mrs Merkel's silence apparently gave some cheer to the American corporate lobbyists, whose activities may actually provide the explanation for it. According to Jan Philipp Albrecht, the rapporteur on the Data Protection Regulation, the Berlin Parliament had been heavily lobbied by US firms on the matter of data protection: 'if you have a large IT company and you don't want a law, you would go to Germany,' he said. Hence, the tapping of Mrs Merkel's phone did serve to raise public perception of data-protection policy, but did not affect the high-level politics as much as one might have expected.

At EU level, concerns about transatlantic electronic surveillance had first been raised in 2000, when a European Parliament report revealed details of a system then known as Echelon.[51] This was a global system originating from the 1970s and developed for the interception of communications, including satellite links, which later evolved into interception of Internet communications. Echelon was set up with the help of the British, under the UK–USA Agreement. In the wake of the Snowden revelations of 2013, the European Parliament once again held a lengthy inquiry into surveillance and the NSA, under MEP Claude Moraes. His report condemned the 'vast, systemic, blanket collection of the personal data of innocent people' and repeated calls for suspension of the 'safe harbor' agreement.[52]

The NSA affair led to some posturing over the forthcoming trade negotiations known as the Transatlantic Trade and Investment Partnership (TTIP). In Germany, public opinion turned against the agreement.[53] The European Parliament's Moraes Report made acceptance of any future trade agreement with the US conditional on full respect for fundamental rights, notably the privacy of individuals. European Commission President Jose-Manuel Barroso said in a speech that questions must be answered by the US authorities in order to rebuild trust:

> TTIP opens a huge potential for both sides. Negotiations on TTIP are and will remain top priority. In parallel, it is important to address concerns that have been clearly expressed on the European side on some intelligence activities and also on the implication for privacy and data protection at European level.[54]

In the face of this European controversy, Ambassador Kennard was summoned to meet EU diplomats. He was confident of being able to work through the issues:[55]

> The flow of data is important to commerce in a very profound way. And so in negotiating a trade agreement, we fully expect that data flows will be part of this negotiation [. . .] What I find discouraging is that some people . . . have raised the spectre that data issues should dominate this discussion at the negotiating table.[56]

For the EU, the sovereignty of data flows referred to by Ambassador Kennard was, of course, the underlying political issue.[57] The new consciousness of the vast scale of surveillance by the US authorities brought with it a fresh understanding of international data flows and how much of European citizens' data could be transferred to the data centres outside the jurisdiction and control of the EU. This implied that safeguards enshrined under EU law could be lost, but it also implied loss of economic control and possibly the draining away of any economic benefits that Europe could hope to gain from its information-society industries. The structural power of the US Internet industries and telecoms providers was embedded in the state's intelligence-gathering operations, and their closeness is illustrated in this case.

The US authorities were lobbied by their industries to intervene in the EU data-protection matter, as shown in this example of testimony to the International Trade Commission:

> The belief on the European side that the United States lacks adequate protections for personal data theoretically could mean that personal data could not be transferred across EU borders to the United States, bringing transatlantic commerce to a grinding halt. To address that unthinkable result, legal mechanisms have been established, to transfer data from the EU to the US. Those mechanisms are costly and burdensome and an unnecessary drag on digital commerce that could be alleviated by the recognition of the US framework as 'adequate' by the European Union.[58]

As we know from the account above, the US ambassador to the EU did intervene. Publicly, it was known that the US had repeatedly expressed concerns.[59] Privately, it was acknowledged that US government sources were contacting the Commission.[60] The ambassador's hidden objective only emerged subsequently.

US officials managed to get hold of a preliminary draft of the proposed Data Protection Regulation from the European Commission in late 2011. The draft, seen by the author, was being circulated within the Commission in order for other directorates to comment on it. This was known in Eurocrat jargon as the 'inter-services draft'[61] and it is standard procedure for all EU laws. The draft included a provision (Article 42), which said data that was subject to a foreign, non-EU court order could not be handed over without the permission of the EU data-protection authorities. Article 42 was intended to protect the data of EU citizens against unreasonable or illegal requests by foreign courts. The text stated: 'No judgment of a court or tribunal and no decision of an administrative authority of a third country requiring a controller or processor to disclose personal data shall be recognized or be enforceable.'[62]

Any data controller receiving such a request would have had to notify the supervisory authority. Clearly, it had implications in the specific context of the NSA surveillance programme because the clause would have forbidden data transfers at the request of US law-enforcement authorities and the FISA court, and so it was dubbed the anti-FISA clause. From the US government perspective, Article 42 was viewed as a blocking statute that would impede the ability of US law-enforcement authorities to access information, for example, in anti-trust cases. It was noted that 'the proposed provisions would conflict with US–EU law-enforcement agreements'.[63] US-based technology companies would not have liked Article 42 either, because it would have put them between a rock and a hard place,[64] carrying a liability risk of having either to turn down requests from the US authorities or break European law by acceding to them.

The inter-services draft prompted a high-pressure campaign coordinated by the US Department of Commerce, aimed at persuading EU policymakers to amend the regulation, a key objective being to drop Article 42. EU Commissioners and their staff were visited by high-ranking US government officials, including Janet Napolitano, Secretary of Homeland Security, and Cameron Kerry, senior legal counsel at the Department of Commerce.[65] The visits were augmented by private, high-level phone calls from senior figures in the US Commerce Department to top-level staff in the European Commission.[66]

Right in the middle of this campaign, Ambassador Kennard made the speech to the Forum Europe Conference cited at the beginning of this chapter – to which, incidentally, he received a terse response from Commissioner Viviane Reding, correcting him on certain points.[67] Mr Kennard is understood to have visited the European Commission President, Jose Manuel Barroso, according to an email released to the advocacy group Access Now under the Freedom of Information Act: 'DG Home is concerned that Barroso's Chief of Staff is friendly with Reding's staff. Amb. Kennard is meeting with Barroso's Chief of Staff tomorrow.'[68]

This diplomatic campaign was accompanied by an 'Informal Note' that had been prepared as a response to the inter-services draft[69] that briefed against Article 42.[70] What is especially revealing, with hindsight, is the comment that 'the Directive will have a detrimental effect on global law enforcement co-operation'. The advocacy group European Digital Rights (EDRi) said that the note was clearly intended to water down the proposed new law:

> Most of the US government objections are rather specious, obviously weak or plain wrong and interest-driven, aiming to water down the standards in the leaked draft regulation. This early-stage intervention obviously aims at reducing interference with access by the US to any data about European citizens in the course of their investigations, showing very little effort to understand the European concept of privacy.[71]

EDRi believed that the calls and the 'Informal Note' may have prompted several Commission services to issue negative internal opinions at the end of the inter-service process. These opinions had to be taken into account by Commissioner Reding's staff before the final proposal could be introduced to the European Parliament. When the regulation was presented to the European Parliament by the Commission on 25 January 2012, Article 42 had mysteriously been deleted. EU officials claimed that in light of the impending EU–US trade talks, such a clause was not expedient. It was reinstated by Mr Albrecht as Article 43a[72] and subsequently adopted in the European Parliament's First Reading. A Freedom of Information Act request from the advocacy group AccessNow indicates that the US authorities continued their lobbying of the EU through 2012, including a high-level briefing to Digital Agenda Commissioner Neelie Kroes. Towards the end of 2012, another briefing paper was prepared, incorporating the heading 'Impact on law-enforcement activities'.[73]

With the luxury of hindsight, it's obvious that the US officials were not playing it straight. They were lobbying as much to protect the availability of European data for intelligence purposes as they were seeking to protect the ability of corporations to move data out to external data centres for processing. The existence of NSA surveillance was known in European policy circles – and this may have prompted the drafting of the anti-FISA clause. However, the full extent of US data-gathering for surveillance in Europe was not known until Edward Snowden released the evidence. One can never be entirely certain, but it is likely that the anti-FISA clause would not have got on the political agenda if it had not been for the Snowden revelations. The US government position coincided with that of the Silicon Valley companies in that both wanted to transfer the personal data of European citizens over to data centres on the other side of the Atlantic. In that regard, the events described in this chapter explain how state interests in surveillance will support corporate interests in Internet businesses that are reliant on data flows. They illustrate how the technology companies hold structural power – *to threaten or preserve security*[74] – and also how the interests of states and corporations may be sufficiently conjoined to override a public interest, even one as important, and emotive, as the right to privacy.

CHAPTER FOUR

Surveillance Liabilities

> The law-enforcement community has engaged with colleagues in European law-enforcement agencies in a number of fora to agree a common data-retention standard. This is a desirable outcome for reasons of mutual assistance and the investigation of cross-border crime. It would also assist the larger, transnational CSPs [communications service providers] in providing a consistent framework to work to.[1]

Here is a British police chief appealing to Parliament for a law that would benefit international telecoms network providers. It is the personification of the state, seeking to gather intelligence and asserting control over the communications infrastructure.[2] Conversely, it indicates the strength of the structural power of the communications providers in areas of security, since it is the political reality that those who hold communications data also have considerable leverage over the state, especially in demanding protection from civil action for helping the state with surveillance activities. The reason why they hold so much power is that surveillance in the Internet era cannot happen without the collection and retention of communications data.

Telephone companies – for fixed and mobile voice telephony – have traditionally helped law-enforcement agencies by supplying data on subscribers and their calls on request. They were able to do so because they kept the data for billing purposes, and frequently held it for quite long periods. AT&T has been cooperating with the US government since the cold-war era in the mid-twentieth century.[3] In the 1990s, BT was understood to hold telephone billing data for up to seven years. In 2010, more than half a million requests for communications data were made by the UK police. This activity fell into the domain of 'covert surveillance'; however, compliance was voluntary. Obviously, in the Internet era, law-enforcement requests are increasingly for Internet-related data such as email and web-browsing records.[4]

The retention of communications traffic data and the authorization of access by law-enforcement and other authorities is highly controversial. If citizens believe the government is snooping, there is a likely chilling effect on free speech and innovation.[5] The retention of most of this data by the network providers is unnecessary for business purposes; hence they are willing to assist governments, but only at a price. According to one Internet industry spokesman: 'Providers will always cooperate – that is characterized as being a responsible citizen. But you don't go looking for things you don't need for serving the customer – that is more like joining the police on a stakeout.'[6]

The chief concern of the network operators involved protection from liability. Network providers do not want to be sued for damages or incur costs resulting from doing the work of the state. Damages may also come in the form of bad public relations. For example, German Internet providers were not happy to be left in the lurch by their government when it emerged that the German intelligence services were intercepting traffic at a large peering exchange of several hundred networks.[7] Here is the problem from the network providers' perspective, as explained by the security expert Glyn Wintle to a UK parliamentary committee:

> There are liability issues all over the house. If I change my systems and, unbeknownst to me, this breaks part of the system and I only find out about it a week later when a request comes in, and I have not logged things for a week, how much money will this cost me? Am I going to face jail time? I hope not – but am I going to face financial costs? Once again, this will act as a big impediment to me changing any part of my system once I have installed it. I would have to

go back and ask you for more money to change a system that
I have already paid for.[8]

The price of the network providers, apart from the costs,
is that the state should put in place laws to provide liability
protection. Their fear was that, in cooperating with the state,
they could become liable for any surveillance that touched on
citizens, with a consequential liability bill that could grow to
billions of dollars. In the US, Section 802 of the 2008 FISA
Amendment Act (FAA)[9] was passed by the US Congress,
apparently in response to pressure from the US telecoms and
Internet industries.[10] Section 802 falls under Title II of the
law, *Protection for Electronic Communications Services Providers*.
It grants immunity from any kind of civil action by their subscribers for assisting with intelligence-gathering activities.
The adoption of Section 802 had been prompted precisely
because of such a liability arising under a class action lawsuit,
backed by the Electronic Frontier Foundation (EFF) against
AT&T. The details in the case papers shed more light on the
real nature of the relationship between the state and the telecoms providers.[11] The plaintiffs alleged that between 2001
and 2006 AT&T had cooperated with the National Security
Agency (NSA) seeking to intercept traffic on the fibre-optic
cables that carried the backbone of the Internet. The key wit-
ness was a former AT&T engineer named Mark Klein.[12] The
court papers alleged violations of the United States Code 50
(USC) 1809, which prohibits electronic surveillance, and of
18 (USC) 2511, which prohibits interception or disclosure of
personal communications.[13] In March 2009, the US government intervened to have the case dismissed by the court, on
the grounds that it could not proceed without compromising
national security.[14]

Following the Snowden revelations of mass surveillance by
the United States National Security Agency (NSA), in 2013, a
law was passed to reform the NSA surveillance activities. This
was the USA Freedom Act,[15] whose proponents claimed that it

ended the NSA's bulk collection of personal data, replacing it
with a more targeted system, whereby data could be obtained
following a specific and justified request. The law also
improved the judicial supervision arrangements for electronic
surveillance requests. Nevertheless, civil liberties groups were
more sceptical as to how effective it would be on implementation. The new system meant that the data would be requested
from the telecoms companies, and hence they would have
to retain and store it. The law arguably had the effect of out-
sourcing the collection and storage of communications data
to the private sector,[16] strengthening their structural power.
Moreover, liabilities would continue to lurk around telecoms
companies who cooperated. In 2015 a fresh lawsuit, filed by
the Wikimedia Foundation and the American Civil Liberties
Union, signalled the ongoing possibilities for legal action with
regard to surveillance. The plaintiffs alleged that the NSA was
intercepting the Internet directly and targeting Wikipedia,[17]
highlighting concerns for the privacy of Wikipedia editors
and for free-speech rights. Whilst the telecoms companies
were not directly addressed by the case, the liability risk was
exposed.

Communications metadata and the EU

The European Union had already put in place a law to protect the liability of the broadband providers in 2005, but it was
struck down by the European Court of Justice (ECJ) in 2014.[18]
That law was the Data Retention Directive, which mandated
the collection and storage of telecommunications traffic data
by the network providers.[19] Its story is a good illustration of
how the state's need for surveillance data can be politically
problematic. In summary, the network providers' need for
liability protection led to a series of political events that mysti-
fied many observers, and, ultimately, a pressured backroom
coup in the European Parliament by the British presidency.
The hurried passage of the law to please the network providers

led to some bad drafting, which ultimately failed to provide sufficient safeguards for citizens and provided the basis for the ECJ decision.

In fact, the Data Retention Directive did not come totally out of the blue. The British government had been putting forward demands for a European policy on the monitoring of electronic communications since the mid-1990s and there were hints in a Council of Ministers document from 1998, which sought access to data including the 'number or other electronic identifier, account number and email address'.[20] Work on data retention had begun in the aftermath of 9/11[21] and a proposal was put forward by the Council of Ministers in 2002, but at the time there was a lack of political will to agree to it.[22]

By 2005, British law-enforcement agencies were keen to establish a data-retention law, claiming that without one there was a serious risk of miscarriages of justice.[23] They claimed that communications data was often the 'only eyewitness account of the crime':[24] 'When a young girl is found dead, the first thing we look for is her phone,' said one Home Office official interviewed by the author in 2005. It was clear that Internet data would be used by law enforcement for crime investigation, and that such use should be governed by law. Interviews with the Hertfordshire police[25] suggested that the storage of telephone data was important for serious crime investigation. It was pointed out that criminals no longer sat at the back of a pub to plan a crime; they could be in the middle of a field with a laptop and a mobile phone. Law enforcement certainly played a part in the creation of the Data Retention Directive, but, as we shall see, they were not the only stake-holders who needed it.

The Data Retention Directive was born in the wake of the 7 July London bombings and the attempted bombing on 21 July 2005. It was also one year after the bombing of four commuter trains in Madrid, in 2004, and therefore a high state of alert was triggered regarding further terrorist attacks in the

EU, ensuring that counter-terrorism went to the top of the scale of priorities. A political justification of fighting terrorism was used to create an urgency for new laws.[26] Contemporary sources suggested that there was an 'atmosphere' of anti-terrorism such that no Justice and Home Affairs minister would dare to say 'no' on an anti-terrorism measure.[27] Hence, the directive was one of a package of measures agreed in July 2005, incorporating an EU Counter-Terrorism Strategy, with an objective of improving cooperation on national security and law enforcement.

The target date for adoption was October 2005.[28] The pressure was tangible. Industry representatives,[29] presenting to the Justice and Home Affairs Council in Newcastle on 8–9 September 2005,[30] said afterwards that it was clear the British presidency had intended to get the legislation approved within its six-month tenure, with officials taking the attitude 'get it through, it doesn't matter if it's vague, we'll deal with it later'.

This may explain, at least in part, why the political process was rushed. The Data Retention Directive went from a draft text to being adopted by the European Parliament in less than six months. That is highly unusual. The former MEP and shadow rapporteur on data retention, Baroness Sarah Ludford, interviewed in 2006 by the author via email, commented that the Civil Liberties Committee was pressured into acting within a very tight timetable 'which arguably makes a mockery of better law-making'.[31] An average gestation time for a directive is about nine months. That allows time for the parliamentary committees to consider it, amendments to be tabled and discussed, and potentially for two readings. Most directives require two readings.

The British government was in charge of the directive's path through the legislature because they held the rotating EU presidency from July to December of 2005, a fact that would have helped it to get the legislation adopted. The presidency chairs the meetings at the Council of Ministers[32] and it has a mandate to set the EU political agenda for its term of office.

Data retention legally fell under Justice and Home Affairs within the EU, which, in British terms, put it within the ambit of the Home Office, and the Home Secretary, Charles Clarke. He framed the case for the law with the twin imperatives of counter-terrorism and fighting crime:

> [T]he tools we are talking about, the telecommunications data we are describing, are vital to investigate and detect terrorism and crime. It is essential, in my view, to provide a propor- tionate and balanced legal basis for the retention of data that would otherwise be erased or anonymized. Variations in data retention practice mean that the ability of investigators and prosecutors to detect and prosecute criminals and terrorists to stop them causing harm, or to catch them after they have caused harm, is dependent on which communications ser- vice provider a suspect, a victim or witness has used or which Member State they were in. That variation gives an open goal to our opponents in criminality, and it is that we are trying to close with this directive.[33]

From early drafts to final text, the Data Retention Directive was criticized for having a poor specification of the data to be retained, as well as weak access controls that would open the way for mass surveillance. The latter was the reason why it was subsequently struck down by the European Court of Justice.[34] It lacked sufficient safeguards to prevent misuse or fraudulent access, over-large requests, 'fishing expeditions' or data-mining. Expert analysts, such as the British computer sci- entist Dr Richard Clayton, said that it was technically flawed.[35] Data-protection experts recommended minimizing the data retained, and ensuring access requests included specification of purpose, with judicial scrutiny on a case-by-case basis.

However, this was many years before Edward Snowden helped the general public to understand how keeping data can be linked to mass surveillance and there was little public debate. The citizens' advocacy groups working on Internet matters were small and underfunded. They had banded together as the nas- cent European Digital Rights (EDRi) group. The situation was different in Germany, where an advocacy group known by the unprepossessing name of Arbeitskreis Vorratdatenspeicherung (Data Retention Working Group) sprang up. According to its advocate, the German lawyer Patrick Breyer, we were facing 'a new dimension in surveillance, as compared to traditional police powers. Data retention does not only apply in specific cases. Instead, society is being pre-emptively engineered to enable blanket recording of the population's behaviour, when using telecommunications networks.'[36]

The original draft text was produced by the Council of Ministers and the intention was to impose it by means of a legal instrument known as a Framework Decision. Following legal advice, the instrument was switched to a Directive,[37] which meant that the European Commission had to draft a new text and the European Parliament was able to scrutinize it. The Commission published a draft directive on data retention on 21 September 2005.[38] What's curious is that there was not much difference between the European Commission's draft Directive and the earlier proposal from the Council of Ministers; indeed, they were remarkably similar.[39] The Commission's job is to draft legislation, but it is not supposed to take a dictated line from the Council.

When the Commission's draft Directive was forwarded to the European Parliament, it was assumed that it would be subject to the process of scrutiny in the usual way. The responsible committee was the Civil Liberties Committee (LIBE), and the Member of the European Parliament (MEP) who had been nominated as rapporteur was Alexander Alvaro, a German Liberal MEP. He had the job of gathering together amendments to the draft Directive and established a political compromise on aspects where there was disagreement. He consulted with industry and privacy advocates, including the nascent EDRi. His proposed amendments incorporated a more limited data-set for Internet data (log and log-off and subscriber details only); a maximum storage time of twelve months and costs to be reimbursed to the broadband providers and phone companies, as well as safeguards on access and retrieval of data, with a requirement for a judicial warrant. Mr Alvaro's report, dated 24 November (prepared in remarkably quick time for such a complex law), was adopted by the Civil Liberties Committee by thirty-three votes in favour, eight against and five abstentions.[40]

In the middle of this process, events began to take an unusual turn. The Civil Liberties Committee received a letter from Charles Clarke. The letter contained a thinly veiled imperative for the European Parliament to fall in line. It expressed a commitment to reaching agreement by the end of 2005, and sought to 'maximize common ground between the Council and the EP on matters of substance, whilst respecting the Council's position'.[41] Mr Clarke additionally tried some megaphone diplomacy in a letter to the *Financial Times* in November 2005, where he argued for 'a consistent approach across Europe'.[42]

At the end of November 2005, Mr Alvaro's report was overturned by the British presidency, breaching process in a manner that is highly unusual. A series of Council working documents from October through to December reveals some manoeuvrings.[43] Firstly, with the Commission at its side, the British presidency sought to bring Mr Alvaro and his committee into back-room talks. These tripartite talks, known as trilogues, are an established procedure in the European Parliament, but it was an unusual step to take during the First Reading of a directive, and prior to the committee agreeing its position. The first trilogue took place on 8 November 2005 and the purpose of the meeting was to discuss possible amendments.[44] Two further meetings occurred on 15 and 22 November 2005.[45] The final trilogue was just two days before the Civil Liberties Committee voted on 24 November.[46]

Mr Alvaro, interviewed by the author in 2006, was upset at the way his report had been treated: 'During the discussions there was a change of paradigm,' he said 'Usually, if you want to breach fundamental rights, you have to justify why you want to do it. We had to justify why we did not want to do it.'[47] He was accused of not supporting the fight against terrorism and confronted by accusations such as 'we know you are bought by industry.' 'I felt they were bullying me,' he said, recalling a conversation with a British official to the effect that 'we want a First Reading agreement and we don't care how'.[48]

It subsequently emerged that a secret deal between the European Parliament and the presidency had been reached on 29 November 2005. Interviewed in July 2006, Mr Alvaro asserted that he did not know how this agreement had come about. He was away for four days on a business trip to Israel between 24 and 29 November and, by the time he returned, he was confronted by an agreement between the Parliament and the Council to back down on his report and to approve the presidency's text. 'I came back and via Reuters I realized there was an agreement between the EPP and the Socialists to accept 100 per cent of the Council amendments [. . .] The Council complained that I was travelling, but I had close contact all the time.'[49]

In a hearing on 7 December 2005, organized by the European Parliament Green Group, Mr Alvaro alleged that whilst he had been absent, the British presidency had held personal meetings with the leaders of the two large party groups.[50] He had been given to understand that the Council had approached the Parliament and not the other way round. He was never informed of their content. In a subsequent interview with the author in 2006, he said:

> I still don't know what the presidency told them. It was after these meetings that the text was swapped back to something very close to the Council's original text. Maybe I was too naïve. I was aware that they may change one or two points, but I did not expect it so quickly, and that it would be 100 per cent of what the Council wanted.[51]

Mr Alvaro's allegation can be substantiated by consulting the records of the debates in the European Parliament. The EPP shadow rapporteur, Ewa Klamt, confirmed that the final text had been agreed 'by the two major groups' whilst the rapporteur was away:

> The rapporteur, Mr Alvaro, may well find this way of going about things to be in bad taste, but it was not possible to reach any agreement with him, as he was not in Brussels during the final stage of the negotiations, but the UK presidency was informed as soon as the two major groups had reached informal agreement on a position, and it was on this basis that agreement in the Council was made possible.[52]

Further confirmation came from Sylvia-Yvonne Kaufmann, speaking on behalf of the Left Group:[53]

> Speaking as my group's shadow rapporteur, let me say that I find it quite simply unacceptable that the two big groups should disregard the Committee's vote and deliberately [– let Mrs Klamt take note of this –] go behind the rapporteur's back and hatch schemes with the Council. The compromise that the PPE-DE and PSE groups have negotiated with the Council is rotten to the core and stinks to high heaven.[54]

The Green Group spokesperson, Kathalijne Buitenweg, reiterated the back-room nature of the deal:

> [As} you have now done a deal with the British presidency before Parliament has even adopted a position, we are now faced with a fait accompli. The small groups were not even informed and even the rapporteur for this subject, Mr Alvaro, knew nothing about this. It is all very well [for Mrs Klamt] to say that they were unable to reach him, but Mr Alvaro has a telephone, and informing the person in question would have been the decent thing to do. What we now have is a back-room deal on citizens' rights.[55]

And finally, Baroness Sarah Ludford, of the Liberal Group, called it a 'con-trick' and a 'sell-out', saying:

> I deplore the attacks on Mr Alvaro; he delivered a resounding near-consensus in Committee. To use his three-day absence on an official trip to Israel at the end of a phone and fax is a cheap alibi for a stab in the back.[56]

Had they done a deal? The desire of the British presidency to do a deal was expressed throughout the autumn of 2005.[57] In order to secure a majority vote, the presidency would have needed the support of the EPP, which was the largest group in the European Parliament. A combination of EPP with the Socialists would be a belt-and-braces approach, making doubly sure that the vote could not be lost. A Council document noted that negotiations were continuing:

> Though the Parliament's willingness and co-operation to hasten the process has been encouraging, there are still divergent views on several key issues between the institutions [. . .] negotiations will continue with the European Parliament in advance of the plenary meeting on 13–14 December.[58]

A final meeting between the presidency and the Parliament was held on 29 November, according to a Council document,[59] and the Data Retention Directive was approved by the Council on 2 December 2005, subject to the Parliament agreeing to it exactly as it stood.[60] That in itself is strange. This was a case of the member-state governments putting on record that adoption of legislation was being dictated to the elected Parliament. On 14 December 2005, it was adopted by the European Parliament, with 378 votes in favour versus 197 against; 30 abstentions and 127 'no votes'.[61] The text was, to all intents and purposes, the British presidency's work and, as Mr Alvaro had noted, it was remarkably similar to its original draft. In particular, the issue of safeguarding access to data had not been addressed, leaving this entirely to national law.[62] But the real question is: who wanted this Directive so much that they pressed British officials to rush it through? Some lobbyists suggest that it was quite simply that the British presidency had produced a 'thin result'.[63] In other words, it was a failure, when measured by the usual EU criteria of the amount of legislation adopted, suggesting that Britain needed this directive to be adopted to salvage its record. But this does not seem like the full answer.

Telecoms lobbyists who were involved at the time[64] say that the network providers were demanding a law to cover their backs for storing communications data when, legally, they had to delete it. The UK had a voluntary data-retention scheme,[65] but a parliamentary committee report had rejected the idea of a mandatory scheme.[66] It's understood that the phone companies – likely to have been Vodafone and BT – had made approaches to British law-enforcement agencies, claiming that the existing data-protection legislation[67] presented a problem for collecting communications traffic data. Their position was that Section 29 of the 2002 Data Protection Act permitted them to release data, provided a sufficient case could be made for it, but this was not compliant with the European Convention on Human Rights (ECHR).[68] Under the Data Protection Act, they had to destroy communications traffic data that was no longer needed for normal business purposes and they were under pressure from their legal compliance managers.[69] In practice, this meant they had to delete or anonymize data, sometimes within twenty-four hours.

Statements to the British Parliament from senior law-enforcement officers backed up this theory. Firstly, the law did not give them the access they wanted to communications traffic data, and they were dependent on the goodwill of the telecoms companies. And, secondly, they could not rely on the data being available in the first place because the telecoms networks were not obliged to retain it, and would, for the above reasons, delete it. The Home Office was still consulting on this matter[70] but law-enforcement authorities were in a hurry for a resolution, stating in evidence to a British parliamentary committee: 'This is untenable, leaving the industry exposed to civil action and law enforcement uncertain of their powers. The law enforcement community urges government to rectify the situation swiftly.'[71]

Law-enforcement chiefs were also demanding a mandatory data-retention scheme, backed by legislation, and they called for it to be done at EU level. Their concern was that waiting for a common EU data-retention legal structure would take a long time and law enforcement could not wait. They urged the Home Office to pursue the idea both at home and in Brussels:

> The law enforcement community [. . .] supports the generality of the work being undertaken by the Home Office to support the EU proposal. The work is at an early stage and is not assured of success. The law enforcement community would urge progress on domestic legislation whist this work evolves.[72]

Hence there was considerable internal and external pressure on the British Home Secretary, which would account for his determination to press the law through Brussels.[73] However, some insiders have hinted that there was an additional source of pressure from the US authorities, which might also explain the excessive keenness of the British to get this law adopted.

An interesting postscript came in 2014, when the law was ruled invalid at the European Court of Justice,[74] which said that the directive failed to guarantee sufficient safeguards under Article 8 of the European Convention on Human Rights[75] (the right to privacy) against unlawful access to the data, and did not have adequate rules for limiting the amount of data stored, the period of time it was stored, and the use of it. The judgment also said that the potential interference with the right to privacy had not been sufficiently circumscribed. Hence, the EU legislators had made some serious mistakes.

The case of the Data Retention Directive illustrates the structural power of the telecoms providers. They have the power to threaten or preserve the security of society. That power is such that states will press on their behalf to get data-retention legislation adopted, even when a law is technically flawed and there is parliamentary opposition – in this case, in the European Parliament. The case provided the political explanation for subsequent laws on both sides of the Atlantic. Communications traffic-data retention remains essential for the state to conduct such surveillance. Laws asking private companies to assist the state only serve to cement the relationship between state and corporations and enhance the industry's structural power, because private actors need immunity from liability when they do the state's dirty work. Hence, the striking down of the Data Retention Directive meant the British government rushed in a new law known as the Data Retention and Investigatory Powers Act 2014 (DRIPA) at breakneck speed, in just two days of parliamentary time, additionally extending the requirement to platform providers of messaging services, and telecoms providers based outside the UK.[76] On a brighter note, a report by QC David Anderson recommended that access to communications traffic data should have judicial oversight.[77] The proposal was – unsurprisingly, because it eases the liability – welcomed by the Internet industry, who gave Anderson the award of 'Internet hero' at their annual dinner.[78]

At the time of going to press, the British government had laid before Parliament a new Investigatory Powers Bill, implementing the Anderson recommendations, with the intention of adopting it within a year.

CHAPTER FIVE

Net Neutrality Under Pressure

One of the best places to see the political power of the large telecoms companies in action is to mingle in the corridors of power where the decisions are being taken. For example, in November 2011, in one of the European Parliament's imposing hemicycles, a policy summit was taking place on the topic of net neutrality.[1] At stake was whether Europe should develop a net-neutrality policy. The seats were filled as an estimated two to three hundred people piled into the room. Any company that considers itself a global player wants to influence Brussels, and the attendee list was a who's who of multinational telecoms companies, including the large European companies such as Vodafone, BT and Deutsche Telekom, and many non-European ones like the American network operators AT&T and Verizon, as well as equipment vendors like Cisco from the US. Even the Chinese manufacturer, Huawei, had sent a representative.

As they laid out their positions in front of the European policymakers, the telecoms industry representatives pleaded that the net-neutrality debate in Europe is about the relationships between commercial organizations and the Internet as we seek sustainable models.[2] It is not, they said, a public infrastructure but a privately funded system. They argued for a sensible position to safeguard the interests of users against the need to preserve the capability of companies to innovate. They warned of the risks of congestion, and why they had to develop ways to manage it. At the same time, they signalled that there was an enormous investment needed to upgrade Europe's telecoms infrastructure. They argued that the law was fine as it stood, and they sought to reassure policymakers that there were 'no legitimate concerns for discrimination' and that 'customers want to consume different volumes of data and to pay prices for different needs'. The sceptic among the observers would have said that the telecoms industry had come to prevent a net-neutrality law in Europe. This chapter discusses the ways in which they seek to influence the political agenda for net neutrality.

Net neutrality is the principle that all traffic is treated without discrimination, restriction or interference regardless of its sender, recipient, type or content.[3] It means that users' freedom to communicate is not restricted by favouring or disfavouring (technically, financially or otherwise) the transmission of specific Internet traffic. The fact that the network operator does not interfere with the traffic and no permission is needed to develop new applications is one of the important reasons why the Internet has grown to what it is today. People can access content from anywhere in the world, and they can publish to anywhere in the world. By implication, they can also trade with anyone, anywhere. The effect of net neutrality means small traders can reach big markets. Small media, for instance bloggers, can compete with big media. It is one of the reasons why democratic speech flourishes on the Internet, and why innovation thrives and trade can expand. Net neutrality means there are no gatekeepers and no tolls. The users choose what they read, see and do, and not the network providers, and, in that regard, net neutrality protects free speech.[4]

At the political level, net neutrality is concerned with interference with Internet traffic and restrictive practices by network operators which have negative externalities.[5] These restrictive practices concern the delivery of services and access to content. There are different ways that restrictions can be imposed. It can be, quite simply, discrimination, where the provider holds back or drops traffic. The motive may be commercial – to make the provider's own services look better and more desirable. Or it may be to act specifically against certain types of traffic, for example for copyright enforcement or parental controls. Another form of interference is throttling, where the traffic is slowed down. This is often done to peer-to-peer file-sharing traffic, making it so slow that the operator hopes to discourage people from doing it. Interference can also be paid prioritization, where, in return for payment, a provider will ensure that certain traffic travels faster and gets priority. Throttling and prioritization are sometimes referred to as the 'slow lane' and 'fast lane' Internet. On a similar principle, the operator may impose bandwidth caps – or limits – and then say that certain content is zero rated, which means it does not count towards the bandwidth limit. This is another form of prioritizing and it is driven by clear commercial motives.

The reason why this becomes an important political issue is that the telecoms industry has dominant control of physical networks. It's a historic dominance, which has been bedded in for well over a century. The very first telephone services were established in the late 1870s in both Europe and America. In France they were established under a government ministry, in Germany they were operated by a postal authority and in Britain they were private companies. These services were the ancestors of today's telecoms networks such as Deutsche Telekom, France Telecom and British Telecom. In America, the long-distance network was built by the American Telephone and Telegraph Company (AT&T), which, in 1899, acquired the Bell telephone companies, and so obtained a monopoly over the US communications infrastructure. That monopoly enabled it to resist any challengers[6] until the regulatory break-up in the 1980s that created the twenty-two regional operating companies, known colloquially as the 'Baby Bells'. The AT&T brand was re-established in 2005, after the long-distance division was purchased by Southwestern Bell. The company now incorporates ten of the former Baby Bells,[7] and this is the AT&T that we know today. With all of these companies, their long history and established networks give them political leverage and, of course, embed their structural power, which they have managed to increase via their broadband networks.

The broadband network providers today control the means of access to knowledge. They can determine by what means and on what terms knowledge is transmitted and received, and the terms of access. They control the below-the-waterline structures of the Internet that provide an essential service.[8] Governments depend on them to fulfil key policy objectives, such as ensuring the universal availability of Internet services. This begins to explain why the telecoms industry did not want net neutrality to be enshrined in law. It did not suit their new business plans to increase revenue. They proposed to do this by slicing up the broadband networks into different services.[9] They were investing in systems to run their networks – known as traffic-management systems – which had the capability to block, slow or throttle traffic, and ultimately enabled the telecoms industry to wield its structural power. For this reason, telecoms lobbyists fought aggressively against net neutrality in the US and the EU.

As a dominant controller of an essential structure, the telecoms industry has been issuing its own demands with regard to net neutrality and has tended to express it as a political choice: either the telecoms providers should be permitted to use traffic management systems as they chose, or they would reduce investment in the network as a whole. They advocated that traffic management would encourage service innovation whereas net neutrality would reduce investment. For example, the European Telecommunications Network Operators (ETNO), representing the large telecoms network operators such as Deutsche Telecom, Telefonica and Telecom Italia, suggested that there would be a shortfall in infrastructure investment, leading to a 'missed opportunity for the broader EU economy', unless the telecoms operators were appropriately 'incentivized'. In this way they appealed directly to the rational interests of the European

Commission by hinting that the broader policy objective of improving broadband infrastructure might not be achieved under a net-neutrality policy:

> a properly reformed regulatory framework can both safeguard competition as well as incentivize the investments in advanced next-generation access networks required for the EU to reach its Digital Agenda targets. [. . .] by 2020 the shortfall in investment needed to meet EU Digital Agenda targets for broadband coverage and penetration will amount to between €110 billion and €170 billion.[10]

ETNO's concept of a 'properly reformed regulatory framework' was to restructure the whole European market, bolstering their dominance by reducing the number of operators, and giving them 'the flexibility to offer differentiated products and services, for example by offering different data volumes, bandwidth limits, and quality of service'.[11] The telecoms industry advocated to EU policymakers that if the industry was prevented from offering differentiated services, this would have a 'negative impact on the investment capacity of the sector'.[12] 'Differentiation' was also taken to mean other non-Internet services that can be delivered over a broadband connection – sometimes also referred to as 'specialized services'. These services could be broadcast television or health services, including video diagnostics or some kind of regular monitoring, such as keeping a check on the heart rate of an elderly person.[13] They could even involve traditional voice telephone. Highlighting the economic benefits, ETNO made the link to infrastructure investment, arguing that the 'additional revenues will improve sustainability of investments and the introduction of innovative functionalities in fixed and mobile internet infrastructure'.[14]

However, the underlying issue was a conflict about who controls the information flows and how the revenues from them will be distributed. The large content platforms, such as Google, Facebook, Skype and WhatsApp (also owned by Facebook), offered new ways to deliver services such as voice,

email and text messaging, in competition with services provided by the telecoms industry. Skype, for example, had more
than 300 million users worldwide, and they are also heavy
users of content.[15] The perception was that these new services
were taking business away from the telecoms companies.
Moreover, people were using new content applications and
services because they were offered free of charge at point of
use. The overall user base for social media services had grown
to some 1.7 billion users,[16] although, as we have seen in chapter 2, these services were not really 'free' – instead, users give
away their data in return for 'free' content and applications,
entering a form of Faustian pact. The content-platform companies tended to have a high market capitalization, and could
be valued at several multiples of the large telecoms network
operators.

For example, in September 2014, Facebook's market capitalization was $200 billion (£127 billion) and Google's was
$400 million (£255 million); Twitter's was $34 billion (£21.76
billion), even though its revenues were only $1.5 billion.[17]
Contrast those figures with British Telecom's market capitalization of £34 billion in the same period.[18] Facebook and
Google had outstripped other technology companies, such
as Hewlett-Packard and Oracle, themselves once the rising
start-ups of their sector. Even more interesting, the market
capitalization of Facebook and Google was higher than the
soft-drinks corporation Coca-Cola. The fingertap of desire (see
chapter 1) had been noted by investors, who saw Facebook as a
low-risk way to tap into the fast-growing mobile market.

The telecoms industry, envious of the high stock-market
valuations of the content platforms, was no longer willing just
to sell a neutral pipe. They perceived the possibility of increasing their revenues through content. They wanted to demand
fees from users, and do deals with content companies. For
example, here is BT speaking to the European Commission:
'We would expect the next three years to see an increase in
existing and new partnerships across the internet value chain

(ISPs, content-providers, mass-storage companies, retailers etc.) to deliver innovative offerings to consumers.'[19]

The fast-lane/slow-lane model evolved into some quite sophisticated forms. BT informed the European Commission that they planned to put their own television services into the fast lane. It proposed to ensure that its television services would receive prioritized treatment on the basis of a contractually guaranteed quality of service – and so it would ensure that the viewer would not be inconvenienced by any network congestion.[20] Whilst this could sound very reasonable, BT and others did not state so clearly that it might mean squeezing the open Internet traffic in order to deliver that contractually guaranteed quality. For example, subscribers who had only one physical broadband connection could find that the available bandwidth for web video or applications would be reduced when the television service was also in use.

More controversial, even among the operators themselves, was the proposal for 'sending party pays'.[21] This was about deals between operators and content platforms regarding the transmission of their services to users. Such payment mechanisms could result in traffic blocking, for example from failure to pay on the part of the sending party, unrecoverable charges incurred by networks, and unwillingness to pay on the part of some over-the-top companies for traffic to less financially viable countries. Hence, entire countries could be cut off from parts of the Internet.[22] A sending-party-pays agreement would result in 'inconsistent and disruptive implementation' as well as selective blocking of content.

This may explain why they came to favour bandwidth caps, with 'zero-rated' content that would not count towards the bandwidth allowance. The zero-rated content would be effectively 'free'; however, if the user accessed content that was not zero rated, they would pay per byte. That could make any competing service very expensive. The zero-rated content would therefore become an offer that the consumer could not refuse.[23] For example, the Canadian operator Bell Network included its own mobile television service as a zero-rated service within a bandwidth cap. A Canadian academic calculated that it would cost a user eight times as much to watch a movie on a competing mobile television service and hence the operator was giving preferential treatment to its own services, making it uneconomic for users to watch the competitors' services.[24] In Europe, the empirical evidence demonstrated that prices for mobile Internet usage rose sharply after operators launched their own zero-rated video services. One European operator zero-rated YouTube videos on its new-launched mobile service, and then tripled the price of open Internet access.[25] Zero rating even extended to Wikipedia, the free Internet-based encyclopedia, which sought to keep itself inside the bandwidth cap.[26]

Another variant was that of so-called 'personalized networking'. This was a proposal to offer different 'app' clouds to each subscriber, whereby business users, professionals and personal users, such as students and families, would each get a differentiated offer based on their usage of software and applications. This kind of offer was enabled by the equipment in the network, using techniques such as deep-packet inspection (DPI), which would enable network providers to know all about their subscribers' online behaviour. DPI equipment is capable of opening packets of data as they travel along on the Internet and examining the data packets on the inside, across the entire network. The data obtained via DPI would be used to add 'intelligence' such as analysis and control of the subscribers, the services and the locations, so they could know in real time who was doing what, when and where, down to the last second and degree of latitude.[27] For example, the network operator could look at everyone walking in Trafalgar Square and know the difference between the young student on Facebook and the middle-aged man in a suit looking up shares, and the other man connecting to his office. They would know this just by looking at the traffic patterns, device, applications, geo-location and content accessed. If they saw that the customer most often accessed social media, for example, they could sell a network access service 'optimized' for social media use. They could also discriminate against content that didn't suit the provider's business model, as this extract from an equipment vendor's promotional video describes:

> From inside the packet core, we get awareness, analysis and control over the network data. You can see what every user is doing on your network, by application, you can divide your users into segments, and sell them more personalized services, for example tailored to social media, or to office connections [. . .] when you see the behaviours you don't like, you can take action [. . .].[28]

EU officials, wanting that network-infrastructure investment to boost other policy goals, seemed to embrace these proposals. Despite the fact that this contradicted the long-term EU policy of building a competitive telecoms market, they were captured by the incumbent line.[29] It reflects the entrenched nature of the telecoms industry's structural power, and can be seen in the way that they lobbied in both 2009, regarding the Telecoms Package, and 2013, over the proposed 'Connected Continent' telecoms regulation.

The telecoms operators advocated to policymakers that these new business models would increase consumer choice'.[30] However, the 'ability to choose' is not the same as being able to access everything and anything. Customers could be choosing from a limited selection chosen by their network provider, and this definition would remain true. It was clear that the industry advocated for rules that would give the network operators the most flexibility, and in this regard they argued that operators should determine how they managed their networks, without regulation.[31] In the US, AT&T fought against an FCC proposal for a net-neutrality rule, even though it allowed for 'reasonable traffic management'.[32] Instead, AT&T proposed that consumers should be informed about any 'material restrictions' – euphemistically calling it 'transparency'. The following extract from an AT&T submission to the Federal Communications Commission (FCC) reflects its position:

> AT&T supports a principle favoring increased transparency about customer-usage limitations as consumers will experience them [. . .] Under this principle, a broadband network operator can and should tell consumers, at an appropriate level of detail, about any material restrictions or limitations on their broadband Internet service so that they can make informed choices about which providers and service plans best meet their needs.[33]

This meant the network provider could implement restrictions, provided they informed the subscriber. Of course, merely telling the subscriber that they were being restricted was a very low legal hurdle, especially without proper regulatory enforcement.

AT&T, together with Verizon and Liberty Global,[34] followed a similar tactic in lobbying the EU during the 2009 Telecoms Package. An AT&T-led alliance, calling themselves the Net Confidence Coalition, argued against any policy which would 'mandate non-discriminatory treatment of network traffic'.[35] They advocated instead for a transparency-and-disclosure rule, very similar to what they proposed to the FCC, where subscribers would be informed 'of any restrictions on their ability to access content or run applications and services of their choice'. Their proposed amendments sought to 'address unjustified degradation of service, usage restrictions and/ or limitations and the slowing of traffic'. In the justification for the amendments, they made it plain that they wanted to ensure that any such restrictions would not be called into question by telecoms regulators – in other words, that restrictions could be a legitimate practice.[36] The law as it stood did not prevent them from doing this, but because it was silent on the matter, it left them exposed to liability claims if they went ahead. This is once again the familiar pattern of a telecoms industry seeking state support for its own protection. But as one observer cynically put it, 'It's OK if they stuff you, as long as they tell you you're being stuffed.'[37]

In fact, the European Commission had attempted to insert a net-neutrality principle into the draft Telecoms Package on 13 November 2007. The provisions were drafted in a way that would have made it difficult for broadband providers to legally block content, by instituting a transparency requirement backed up by a quality-of-service requirement, and an obligation on regulators to protect users' rights to access content, services and application. These provisions were in turn backed up by a possibility for the European Commission to intervene.[38] The rationale was described in the accompanying Impact Assessment.[39] However, two things happened during the EU political process. These provisions, which had been carefully crafted by the European Commission, were dropped by the European Parliament. They were replaced by amendments reflecting AT&T's preference for 'meaningful transparency'. As part of a political compromise, the language of 'restriction' was changed to 'conditions limiting access to and/or use of content, services and applications'. The compromise provision stated that it 'neither mandated nor prohibited' such conditions, but did provide for information about them.[40] In practice, this was interpreted to mean that it did not forbid broadband providers from blocking or traffic-shaping practices, as long as they informed subscribers. The information could be provided in the subscriber contract, or in subsequent information sent to the subscriber. This was exactly what the telecoms industry wanted. However, in this instance, events intervened, and although they did not change this particular provision in the law, they did move net neutrality on to the EU agenda. A public campaign led to a deluge of emails from the public all over Europe,[41] and when the law was finally adopted on 4 November 2009,[42] the Parliament also drafted the Net Neutrality Declaration, which mandated the Commission to put it on the policy agenda. This led to the Net Neutrality summit described at the beginning of this chapter.

The next development was in July 2013, when it emerged that the EU European Commission was working on a new piece of legislation that addressed net neutrality within the wider context of telecoms regulation. This time it was an open secret that the law had been drafted under pressure from the telecoms industry, with the European coalition represented by ETNO taking the lead.

There had been no public consultation, representing a breach of process. There were at least three leaked drafts dated 11 and 15 July 2013 and 28 August 2013. All three preliminary drafts indicated a position on net neutrality that would have allowed network providers to prioritize paid-for content.[43]

This was confirmed when the legislation was officially presented on 11 September 2013. The proposed new law was called the 'Connected Continent'[44] Regulation. The significance of it being a regulation was that it would immediately apply in all EU member states, whereas a directive would have permitted options on implementation. This added to its controversy.

The 'Connected Continent' Regulation was accompanied by a fanfare of press announcements that the EU would protect net neutrality. 'The legislation proposed today is great news for the future of mobile and internet in Europe. The European Commission says yes to net neutrality,' announced Neelie Kroes, European Commissioner for the Digital Agenda.[45] In the political context as described above, it becomes easier to see the ways in which the text was deceptively drafted. The 'Connected Continent' proposal seemed to have incorporated the industry's policy agenda, which proposed to use deep-packet inspection for 'product differentiation'.[46] The text embedded the structural power of the telecoms providers to impose prioritization of traffic. It would not only have supported the use of traffic management, but also industry demands for restructuring in an anti-competitive manner. The proposed restructuring would have underpinned the near-monopolies of some of the big European stakeholders such as Deutsche Telekom and Telefonica, a move which would have put considerably more structural power into a very few hands.

Regarding net neutrality, the Commission had disallowed blocking of Internet content, but did permit 'reasonable traffic-management' measures to 'minimize the effects of network congestion'. However, it explicitly permitted price differentiation and bandwidth caps, using the wording 'contractually agreed data volumes and speeds'. The text was interpreted by many experts as permitting prioritization of the operator's own services under a quality-of-service agreement,[47] and so it would have opened the way for content-related deals. It could have enabled prioritization or zero rating of content under agreements with content, services and application providers.[48] It would have allowed providers to impose terms that would have the effect of restricting usage to just those content sites and services approved by the provider, and/or which had a financial deal with the provider, although they would not have been allowed to call it 'Internet access'.[49]

Subsequently, the European Parliament overturned the Commission's proposals, swayed again by the volume of emails it received from concerned citizens, and adopted the principle of net neutrality by incorporating a definition into the proposed law[50] in its First Reading on 3 April 2014: '"Net neutrality" means the principle according to which all internet traffic is treated equally, without discrimination, restriction or interference, independently of its sender, recipient, type, content, device, service or application.'[51]

The adoption of this and other supporting amendments established a political red line, and it also created a significant political divide between the Parliament and the Council of Ministers, the body that represents the governments of all twenty-eight member states. The Council was also split internally between those member-state governments that had already passed positive net-neutrality laws and those whose telecoms incumbents would oppose such a law. The

Netherlands and Slovenia, with net-neutrality laws, would have benefited from one in the EU. As far as could be seen, they were supported by Estonia, Poland, Greece, Hungary and Finland. On the opposite side were the British, hamstrung by their broadband providers who were being asked to filter content (see chapter 6) and, as a consequence, would oppose a net-neutrality law. The wider political debate over net neutrality was mirrored in the internal political struggle in the Council, which somehow had to come to an agreement between the two polarized positions. It was clear that some members of the Council were keen to support the telecoms industry position and in favour of permitting paid prioritization through traffic management, and that there was a will to accommodate the British. It was also clear that such a position would have difficulty getting a consensus, which is the norm for the Council.

In the midst of the EU deliberations, there was a significant development in the US, when, on 4 February 2015, the Federal Communications Commission (FCC) came out with proposed new rules for protecting the open Internet. This was not the first time that the FCC had ruled on net neutrality. In 2008, the FCC had ruled against Comcast for throttling competitors' traffic, and in 2010 it had issued an Open Internet Order, which specified no blocking or unreasonable discrimination and ordered transparency on the part of the network operator. The Open Internet Order had underlined that the violation of the open Internet may cause harm that is substantial, costly and in some cases potentially irreversible.[52] In 2014, in a legal challenge from Verizon, the US Court of Appeal ruled that the FCC had overreached its powers. The court had said that the FCC did not have the authority to impose the order, but that it could mandate the network providers to tell subscribers about their traffic management.[53] The FCC Chairman, Tom Wheeler, responded with a commitment to protecting the Internet as a channel for innovation and free speech.[54] Just before his February 2015 announcement, Mr Wheeler won support from US President Barack Obama – who called for no blocking, no paid prioritization, no throttling[55] – and he received around 4 million emails from citizens. The FCC's February 2015 order mandated that the broadband providers be reclassified as common carriers, under Title II of the 1996 US Telecommunications Act, which would allow the FCC to ensure the Internet remains open, on fixed and on mobile networks.

The US telecoms industry warned that the government was making a 'mistake' and that regulating the Internet as a common carrier was a case of '1930s utility-era regulation applied to the Internet' that would have a negative effect on investment. In a classic illustration of how corporations use structural power as a political lever, AT&T retaliated by threatening to withhold investment in fibre networks for super-fast broadband in 100 US cities.[56] Chairman Wheeler hit back with a letter asking if AT&T had changed its mind about the profitability of investing in fibre.[57]

Back in the EU, the telecoms industry could not help but show its annoyance with the perceived negative results of a process that it had sought to control. AT&T informed the European Commission that it would withdraw investment if a net-neutrality law was passed. ETNO continued to demand unregulated traffic management with thinly veiled hints that, without it, there would not be the funding for network infrastructure development:

> We need balanced rules on traffic management as well as measures that allow the development of specialized services and innovative offers. Only in this way can we ensure high-quality user experience, provide consumers with innovative services and make sure that no economic actor is prevented from developing new business models.[58]

The initial response from the EU Council of Ministers leaned towards the telecoms industry line. The Council put forward an opaquely worded draft proposal that claimed to establish a 'principles-based' approach,[59] but the principles related primarily to traffic management, not net neutrality. The Council's preferred approach was similar to the Commission's original proposal. It sought flexibility for network providers, which would be banned from discriminatory practices, such as blocking or throttling, but would be permitted to use 'reasonable traffic management', and to offer some form of favoured content and 'specialized services'. The Council maintained this approach in a series of drafts that appeared during the period from November 2014 to July 2015.[60]

However, in 2015, there was pressure to conclude a political agreement between the three EU institutions – Council of Ministers, Parliament and Commission. They began 'trilogues' with the aim of speeding up the process and an agreement was released on 8 July. The complex wording of the text is difficult to unpack, even for experts. The Parliament's net-neutrality amendments had been deleted, and instead the agreement defined in some depth what operators may or may not do using traffic management. The trilogue agreement did not allow operators to discriminate against content, or throttle traffic or offer paid prioritization. That much was clear. It was also clear that the agreement did not permit monitoring of content, and that it called for all traffic-management practices to be necessary and proportionate and compliant with European Union law, which includes compliance with the European Convention on Human Rights. Under this agreement, traffic management should also not be based on commercial considerations, which would also seem to preclude any kind of content deals. Specialized services were permitted, but should not be used to circumvent the open Internet. All of those provisions would support a net-neutrality perspective. On the other hand, a particular difficulty with the trilogue agreement was its position regarding zero rating. It was unclear whether or not zero rating would be permitted or not, and opinion was divided as to the intention.

Ultimately, experts on both sides were not entirely happy

with the agreement. Net-neutrality experts said that, whilst the agreement was imperfect, it did contain a number of positive provisions and would go some way towards protecting net neutrality in Europe.[61] On the other hand, some industry lawyers complained that it was an 'unusual intervention into commercial business models in the sector', although they believed that it still left scope to develop prioritized business models.[62]

Views remained divided when the agreement was adopted into law on 27 October 2015. However, telecoms industry reaction indicated that zero rating was permitted. Irrespective of the final outcome, this case illustrates how the telecoms industry will challenge any move by policymakers in favour of a positive net-neutrality law. Only by understanding the underlying agenda for the technology and the control of the infrastructure can we identify the real issues and successfully challenge the more spurious and meretricious industry arguments. This chapter has only provided a short summary of what is in reality a very complex and technically difficult debate. However, the same arguments tend to be reiterated in order to pressure policymakers and they are likely to continue for some time. The big telecoms corporations not only have the power to control access to information, using traffic-management systems – *to accede or deny access to knowledge*[63] – but they exercise it by attempting to shape the political agenda.

CHAPTER SIX

Filtering Policy

> Industry wants assurance that Government is
> comfortable that the proposed legislation doesn't
> conflict with UK practices.[1]

The 'industry' in this quote consisted of the four largest British
Internet service providers and the 'practices' referred to a content-filtering system that they had been asked to implement
by the government. They had become concerned about a proposed European net-neutrality law (chapter 5) that threatened
to render their actions illegal, and their response was to ask
the UK government to block the changes in Brussels. It was
an instance where the state had sought help from industry,
but the public-policy demands had created a liability risk, and
the network providers had pushed the state to cover for them.
The aim of the policy was to prevent children from viewing
pornographic content on the Internet, a policy aim to defend
the rights of children with which few would disagree. The
filtering system was intended to provide 'parental controls'.
However, the purpose of this chapter is to discuss the conflict of rights created by the way in which the filtering system
was implemented, and the responses of the private actors
involved. Content-filtering is an instance where the structural
power of the network providers is exercised by denying access.
Filtering creates interference in the deeper levels of the network, and its aim is to determine what we may and may not
see, read or interact with. It affects the rights of both the information or e-commerce provider and the receiver. It arguably
engages with our very soul. From a public-policy perspective,

content-filtering is a form of censorship, even where the policy aim is laudable and supported by sound and acceptable reasoning. For those reasons, content-filtering is arguably the most serious of all Internet restrictions, and should only be carried out where necessary, proportionate and prescribed by law, and overseen by the judiciary. This means, therefore, that the position of private corporate actors engaging in filtering is fraught with legal uncertainty, edging into human rights law as well as commercial and telecoms law. Content-filtering is contentious because, by definition, it requires Internet service providers to examine all communications in order to identify and remove the objectionable elements. In order to be effective, a filtering system must be systematic and universal. A filtering system comprises hardware units that can monitor and examine the traffic, and software that checks the traffic to determine whether or not the content is permitted to be viewed or accessed by an individual subscriber. If the subscriber is not permitted, then the hardware puts in place the diversion mechanisms, which may be as simple as letting the data packets drop.

The hardware implementation is effected using the heavy artillery of the Internet, systems known as 'deep-packet inspection' (DPI), which are capable not only of opening up every single data packet, but of selecting packets relating to each and every individual user and determining whether to permit that traffic to continue, or not. Deep-packet inspection systems can identify the protocols used by different applications and so the provider can 'see', for example, who is playing online games or file-sharing. The latest systems can go right into the application layer, to classify content and extract metadata. Traffic can be intercepted, inspected, directed and transformed. Content-filtering provides the criteria for the DPI system to determine what it should do with the traffic.[2]

Content-filtering systems check the files and applications that have been identified by the DPI system against a set of predefined criteria on a database. These databases are vast lockers of website pages and their addresses, classified into categories according to what is allowed or what should be blocked. The blocking may be carried out the same way for all subscribers by implementing it on the network routers; it effectively removes content that is not permitted. Alternatively, it is possible for the filtering and blocking to be done at the level of the individual subscriber, in which case the filtering system will hold a database of the websites and services which a subscriber is permitted to see, and will screen against it all of the pages that the user tries to access. It prevents that individual from accessing the banned content, but leaves it visible to others. In such cases, the content-filtering system has to be implemented by the Internet service providers at the point where they control the Internet access for each subscriber. Hence, a content-filtering system will monitor every packet of data transmitted by a user, in order to find the content they are not supposed to see. This is the method used in network-based parental-control systems in the UK. It's also the method used in Russia to implement political censorship.

Filtering systems have been addressed in the European courts, in the case of Scarlet Extended. This case concerned a small Belgian Internet service provider being sued by a music collecting society, demanding that it should filter out all content that belonged to its repertoire. The ruling of the European Court of Justice (ECJ), in 2011, has become the red line in terms of what may or may not be done legally. EU law says that Internet service providers are mere conduits,[3] meaning that they do not need to know or care what content they are carrying. It also says that Internet service providers may not be given a 'general obligation to monitor'.[4]

The notion of 'general monitoring' is an important legal distinction highlighted by the Scarlet Extended case. The ECJ said that EU law does not permit an injunction that requires a telecoms provider to filter 'indiscriminately, to all its customers, as a preventative measure, exclusively at its expense, and for an unlimited period'.[5] Effectively, this means that a general

obligation to monitor is anything involving continuous monitoring, of all content, for unlimited periods of time. Based on
those criteria, a filtering system that monitors all subscribers,
all of the time, as a preventive measure, is a general monitoring system[6] and would not be permitted. This does not
preclude filtering measures being ordered, but there are
strict legal criteria that a filtering order should meet. Filtering
measures must be necessary and proportionate; they should
be targeted, and the determination of the filtering criteria or
the content to be filtered should be ordered by a court or a
body independent of political influence, and should be subject to judicial oversight. In addition, such measures should
not impose excessive costs on the broadband providers.[7] The
law does permit injunctions asking ISPs to block specific content that is deemed to be unlawful, but there are restrictions
placed on the type of injunction that may be granted. It must
be narrow in scope and specific to the aim.[8] Injunctions have
been used for copyright enforcement (see chapter 8). There is
also a reminder in EU telecoms law that national measures to
restrict the Internet must be subject to a prior, fair and impartial hearing – the so-called 'Internet Freedom' provision.[9]

However, in this chapter, we are talking about systems
implemented by the broadband providers under a 'voluntary'
or 'self-regulatory agreement'. Self-regulatory implementation
of content-filtering poses a number of different legal issues
and arguably would not meet the standards set by the Council
of Europe, the body that oversees the European Convention
on Human Rights (ECHR), to which Britain and all other EU
member states are signatories, and which is enshrined in EU
law.

Under the ECHR, Articles 8 and 10, governments have a
duty to guarantee the rights to freedom of expression and the
right to privacy 'without interference from a public authority'. While neither of these rights is absolute, any attempt to
restrict them must fall within categories that may properly
trigger a restriction within the context of the ECHR,[10] and

such a restriction must be necessary, proportionate and prescribed by law. The EU has also developed and adopted its own Charter of Fundamental Rights, which additionally enshrines a freedom to conduct a business (Article 16).[11] Under EU law, all three of these rights would have to be taken into account, and the law has to find the most appropriate balance. The rights of persons for whose benefit the filtering is being conducted – who may be children, for example – would also have to be within that balance.

Filtering, which involves the monitoring of individual communications and subsequently blocking access to content, is recognized for its ability to interfere with both privacy and freedom of expression.[12] One form of interference may occur due to the choice of filtering criteria. For example, an overzealous blocking move by a US government-sponsored service managed to block its own embassies by blocking all domains containing the word 'ass', including 'usembassy.state.gov'.[13] As the blocking is entirely automated, there is no possibility for human intervention in such cases. This problem of blocking legitimate content in addition to the banned content is known as over-blocking.

In *Yildirim* v. *Turkey* – a case of over-blocking – the European Court of Human Rights made it clear that there must be a strict legal framework to regulate any ban on content and states must also guarantee the possibility of a judicial review to prevent abuses of measures that constitute possible interference. In detail, its ruling states:

> blocking access to the Internet, or parts of the Internet, for whole populations or segments of the public can never be justified, including in the interests of justice, public order or national security. Thus, any indiscriminate blocking measure which interferes with lawful content, sites or platforms as a collateral effect of a measure aimed at illegal content or an illegal site or platform fails per se the 'adequacy' test, in so far as it lacks a 'rational connection', that is, a plausible instrumental relationship between the interference and the

social need pursued. By the same token, blocking orders imposed on sites and platforms which remain valid indefinitely or for long periods are tantamount to inadmissible forms of prior restraint, in other words, to pure censorship.[14]

On that basis, the prospect of national measures for filtering of Internet content crashes right up against these finely drawn balances between free speech and other rights, and raises the spectre of Internet restrictions and censorship. There are tensions between rights of the intermediary to conduct business, and the freedom of expression and privacy rights of the individual Internet user, as well as the rights of others (where others could be children in this context, or they could be copyright-holders). Even if general monitoring were permitted, it would violate the competing rights of the intermediary and its customers.

A filtering policy would create difficulties where private actors are asked to implement it, because they may be expected to exercise a quasi-legal judgment in multiple cases, and they are not set up or competent to act as content censors.[15] Such decision-making requirement would impose risk and uncertainty, potentially exposing them to liabilities under civil law. Where content-filtering is network-based, the system may be implemented by the Internet service providers at the point where they control the Internet access for each subscriber. It means that they will monitor the web-browsing traffic of all of the subscribers all of the time, looking for banned pages as defined by their own filtering criteria. From a public-policy perspective, the way that those criteria are determined is important. Notably, the criteria for determining whether a webpage should be blocked, and on what basis the decision is taken, should be made public so that individual users can determine for themselves, before they upload anything, whether or not it breaches those criteria. Where the content-filtering software is developed and provided by outsourced, third-party companies, there should be full transparency and accountability for the way the classification is carried out, and how the criteria are determined. If this work is done behind corporate doors, there can be no accountability of any sort.

The British government began to consider the idea of network-level filtering for parental controls as a policy response to the 2011 Bailey review[16] on the sexualization of childhood, published by the Department for Education. One of its fourteen recommendations was that Internet providers should 'develop effective parental controls'. Since then, further evidence that there is a policy issue regarding children looking at inappropriate content online has been established by the EU Kidsonline project.[17]

The British policy rationale was originally intended to address the possibility of children being able to access adult pornography, and to prevent children from being able to view inappropriate sexual content (as distinct from the issue of child pornography, which is legally classified as child abuse, is a criminal offence and is addressed by law-enforcement means). Round-table discussions began with industry in 2011.[18] However, Internet industry insiders claim that the government changed the policy aim from protecting children from viewing pornography to 'material inappropriate for children', allegedly out of civil-service prudishness. Whatever the reason, this broadening of the policy aim implied a much larger spread of content to be filtered and arguably risked violation of ECHR rights. It was pointed out to the author rather bluntly that 'the idea that this is being done by a barrister versed in human rights law – of course not!'[19]

The broadening of the policy would seem to be substantiated by what we know about the system implementation. This was a commercial secret until it was revealed in a 2014 court ruling[20] that gave details of the network-filtering systems for parental controls, as operated by the four major broadband providers. BT has a system from Nomimum. TalkTalk has purchased its system from Huawei, the Chinese equipment manufacturer. Virgin has the WebSafe system. The court ruling does not detail the name of the supplier, and an online search reveals two vendors with a product called Websafe,[21] so it is not clear where the system comes from and who might be determining its criteria. Sky has a system called SkyShield, but it is not clear who the supplier is. Technically, the systems use three methods of blocking: DPI-based web-address blocking, IP-address blocking and DNS blocking. The ruling does not detail how these systems determine the filtering criteria, but does state the number of categories used by each: BT has seventeen, Sky has ten, TalkTalk has nine and Virgin has eight. It is immediately obvious that all are working to different numbers of categories and it can be inferred that they differ in their definition of the type of content to be blocked and the criteria for selecting the individual pages. The categories go much wider than just 'adult' sites to include drugs, guns, copyright enforcement, anorexia and bullying. BT's Nominum system, for example, includes gambling, social networking and games when blocking individual websites. Hence, a policy that had begun with a genuine desire of the Conservative-Liberal Democrat coalition government to do something to protect children from viewing pornography on the Internet, had apparently acquired mission creep.

Policy discussions took place between the British government and selected stakeholders from 2011 until 2014. These discussions were hosted by government ministries: the Home Office, Education, and Culture, Media and Sport were all involved. The four major ISPs – BT, Virgin, Sky and TalkTalk – who had undertaken to implement a content-filtering system were all represented. So were the mobile operators, who had also implemented network-level filtering for parental controls. In addition, the talks brought in manufacturers of smartphones plus the large content platforms, and representatives of children's charities. This was therefore quite a large group. From what can be ascertained, these meetings did not form part of a public consultation but they do appear to have influenced the policy decision-making process. There is some evidence of industry manoeuvring the policy to suit their own interests (noting that an industry representative attending a meeting at a government ministry is there solely to represent his or her company's interests). It seems there was little, if any, discussion on the possible harms of network-filtering technologies. Indeed, there was concern to keep matters quiet in the public context, including a bizarre reference to the national security committee COBRA,[22] which meets in secret. However, the minutes of the meetings have been made public. Those minutes have made it possible to gain some insights into the process, and form the basis of this account.

According to published minutes, discussions at these meetings addressed issues including the progress of filtering implementation, content classification and the technologies to which the filters would be applied, for example, public WiFi.[23] Smartphone manufacturers were pressed to come up with a filtering solution.[24] It was considered that 'there has never been a better time to be able to "fix" content: filtering products have changed dramatically'.[25] Gender issues and protection of girls and women on the Internet were considered, as well as terrorism and extremism, in moves that were consistent with the broadening of the policy aims.[26]

Of particular interest in a structural power context was the issue of over-blocking. The minutes record how this issue was addressed by a subgroup. The group seemed primarily concerned with minimizing the effect: 'the number of reported incidences of over-blocking appears to be low and the number of valid over-blocks lower still'.[27] This was a surprising attitude in light of the potential for engagement of the privacy and free-speech rights. The subgroup was chaired by a representative of an organization called the Family Online Safety Institute (FOSI). This is a Washington-based organization, with a membership comprising global Internet or telecommunications corporations.[28] In July 2015, its members included AT&T, BT, Verizon, France Telecom Orange, Vodafone, Google, Facebook and the Motion Picture Association of America, as well as content-filtering vendors – Symantec and Nominum.

The member companies evidently have an interest in the evolution of policy on Internet restrictions and content-filtering, and there are some whose financial interests could be directly served by it. Might they benefit from a harmless public perception of over-blocking and would they have an interest in playing down the possibility for violation of freedom of expression? It begs the question as to the real interest of these companies in the UK government parental-controls policy and, noting that the Civil Service Code has strict rules governing contact with lobbyists, it is unclear why this was allowed to happen in a committee that was chaired by a government minister.[29]

The implementation of the filtering system has raised further question marks regarding over-blocking. A project by the Open Rights Group, still in beta test at the time of writing, reported blocking rates of 5–13 per cent of all websites tested across the four major ISPs and the four mobile network operators.[30] Instances of over-blocking have been reported, including a *Guardian* article about a new school for lesbian and gay children being blocked by a mobile operator.[31] Another report suggested that a plug-in called jQuery, used by thousands of websites, had been blocked by one of the major ISPs.[32] It is arguable that the content-filtering implementation counts as 'national measures', that they impose a form of general monitoring, and that they engage the rights to freedom of expression and privacy under the European Convention on Human Rights. On that basis, it would seem that the network providers were in an exposed position.

The concern here is not with the policy aim, which is entirely laudable. Clearly, it is inappropriate for children to view pornography, some of which is highly offensive and distasteful. Academic research has found that children themselves tell how they struggle with risks online.[33] It should also be noted that this is a separate issue from the blocking of child sexual abuse images online,[34] which is addressed by criminal law: that such images should be blocked is not disputed. The concern here is with certain players in the Internet industry and whether, having agreed to implement this policy, they colluded in order to avoid public debate around the negative externalities of content-filtering.

The broadband providers operated the filtering system under a self-regulatory process with a 'voluntary agreement'. From a legal perspective, it meant they were operating it without the backing of a law to protect them from liability, for example, the possibility of civil-law allegations of over-blocking. The 'voluntary agreement' covered the four largest fixed-broadband providers, and the mobile networks who implemented network-level filters for content controls to meet the policy objective of preventing children viewing inappropriate content. However, the government wanted the filtering to be installed as the default for all subscribers, even for adults over eighteen: an unavoidable choice. The industry resisted this demand because the liability risk would have been too high. They worked round the problem by putting a box that is pre-ticked so that, if the subscriber did nothing, their Internet service would be filtered with full child protection.[35] The subscriber who did not untick the box had 'requested' the filters. If the subscriber unticked the box, they got the unfiltered Internet. Some providers offered subscribers the option to check through a list of categories and say whether they would like it to remain filtered or to have access to it. This would be optional, and may be two or three clicks away from the initial page. From a civil liberties perspective, it presented the risk that if people were not supplied with a full list of criteria, they would not be fully informed and hence unable to make any kind of judgement as to whether or not they would like the filtering turned on. Some mobile network operators, such as Vodafone, nevertheless put the filtering on as a default and insisted that subscribers request to have it taken off.[36]

On talking to representatives of the British Internet service providers, they argued that there is no legally enforceable right on the part of the provider to protect free speech. They claimed that mere conduit is a shield against attacks from third-party industries such as the entertainment industries, but there is no requirement for them to be a neutral carrier, and if they choose not to be, there is no way of challenging that. They further state that they have no obligation to carry any given content.[37] They asserted that: 'Unless there is a clear requirement established by law on the providers, it could be very difficult to mount a legal challenge. That is what the Internet Service Providers have been counting on. That the E-commerce Directive should support this[38] is not a position that legal advisors to the ISPs will agree with.' This is why others would argue that a net-neutrality law is needed.

From what can be ascertained, the government insisted that the industry should agree to implement this filtering and gave them little choice. Industry insiders have described a tense meeting with the former culture minister Maria Miller, with the media being briefed outside the room.[39] Hence, the notion of the measure being 'voluntary' would seem to be in word but not in spirit.

It was therefore unsurprising that the large broadband providers – mobile and fixed – wanted the government to oppose European proposals for net neutrality. This was the proposal for a new European telecoms regulation, known as the 'Connected Continent'[40] (see chapter 5) A net-neutrality law would be incompatible with the broadband providers' content-filtering systems. Drafts of the proposed regulation leaked out of the European Commission from July to September 2013. The text did contain an explicit ban on blocking content by network operators. However, experts were able to see through the leaked texts how the Commission's thinking was evolving. One notable difference between a draft dated 11 July 2013 and another one dated 28 August 2013 was the inclusion of an exception for 'voluntary actions of providers to prevent access to and exceptional distribution of child pornography'.[41] The same text appears in the final version.[42] In other words, networks would not be permitted to discriminate against particular types of content, with the exception of those operating this kind of filtering system. It is curious that the inclusion of this sentence – which clearly addresses the British position – occurred not long after a meeting chaired by the Minister of State for Culture and the Digital Economy, Ed Vaizey. He had called for 'a focus on the problems which can be solved internationally and care should be taken to ensure that the issues of net neutrality and freedom of expression are set aside [sic]',[43] and it was agreed that he should write to the European Commissioner.

On 3 April 2014 the European Parliament voted in an amendment to the 'Connected Continent', adding a positive net-neutrality provision: '"net neutrality" means the principle according to which all internet traffic is treated equally, without discrimination, restriction or interference, independently of its sender, recipient, type, content, device, service or application'.[44]

This provision did not suit the British telecoms operators, because it sought to enshrine a net-neutrality law. Can it be a coincidence that – according to Brussels insiders – just forty-eight hours before the Parliament voted, a telephone campaign was orchestrated to influence MEPs that the net-neutrality amendments would be harmful to children?[45]

This brings us back to the quote at the beginning of this chapter, which is taken from the minutes of a meeting on 9 September 2014. The British broadband operators had sought assurance from the government that this proposed EU legislation would not conflict with their filtering practices. The minister, Ed Vaizey, responded that the government was 'talking to the Commission to ensure these concerns are front of mind'. This suggests that the British government had been lobbying at EU level on behalf of the broadband providers. The meeting minutes record a general note regarding the discussion that must have taken place, confirming an understanding that a 'default on' filter would be legally problematic:

There has been some talk that the proposed regulation may hinder the work of the group, but EV didn't believe this to be the case. Net neutrality is a hugely emotive issue, MEPs clearly support work by the Commission, but it shouldn't affect our work – it won't stop us removing images that are clearly illegal, and optional filters won't be affected. [. . .]. We have a voluntary code in the UK because we support a definition of net neutrality which means that ISPs shouldn't block competitor services, e.g. Skype. We want to leave room for the market to innovate. [. . .] There are three issues: i. clean feeds – of small concern; ii. parental controls in the home – this is consensual so not a problem (unless they were default on); iii. public Wi-Fi – this is more worrying as it blocks legal content by default – so this could be a problem.[46]

Arguably, this quote suggests that the British Internet service providers, having agreed to implement filtering on a 'voluntary' basis, knew they were treading on shaky legal ground.

An analysis of the discussions that followed in 2015 in the Council of Ministers suggests that the Council was seeking to accommodate a position for the British government in support of the network providers. At one point, the text gave an exception for filtering where users had requested the service themselves[47] and clarified that this could relate to a parental controls function.[48] However, the exception was dropped as part of the political agreement between the Council, Parliament and Commission[49] of July 2015.

Ultimately, this case highlights the structural power of the networks. They possessed the ability to accede and deny access to content via their control of the network infrastructure, and that was their bargaining chip. The case illustrates how measures implemented by private actors appear desirable from the state perspective, but they may result in negative externalities being covered up and significant structural power being entrenched by corporate actors who will seek to use their leverage in pressuring the state to accede to their own demands.

CHAPTER SEVEN

The Cooperation Agenda

IFPI estimated in 2006 that there are 20 billion illegal downloads of music files each year, far outstripping the developing legitimate digital market and presenting enforcement challenges for rights-holders. Developing cooperation with ISPs to address illegal downloads is key to the future of the music business.

This cooperation has not been sufficiently forthcoming from ISPs in Europe so far. In general, ISPs do not cooperate with rights-holders in the specific circumstances where infringing content is hosted on their own servers, by removing or disabling access to content in response to a notice [. . .][1]

The cooperation agenda is about restricting access to content in order to address allegations of copyright infringement. As the quote above illustrates, the entertainment industries, led by the recorded music and movie companies, demanded that the broadband providers should police their networks on behalf of copyright owners – in other words, that networks such as BT or TalkTalk, Deutsche Telekom or Orange, could be asked to take action against alleged infringers. They wanted the providers to use the technology in the middle layers of their networks to block content that infringed copyright or, alternatively, disconnect subscribers who downloaded infringing material. This is what they termed 'cooperation' – a word that occurred repetitively in rights-holder submissions to governments.[2] In the citation above, which comes from a memo circulated by the International Federation of Phonographic Industries (IFPI), representing the major music labels, to Members of the European Parliament in 2007, the music industry is asking for the network providers to disable access to content – in other words to block it. In the following citation, drawn from a document submitted to the European Commission, IFPI uses the same type of language to ask specifically for content-filtering: 'with cooperation from ISPs, technology and filtering measures can be used to support and supplement enforcement by rights-holders thereby to some extent shifting focus away from individual lawsuits'.[3]

From a structural-power perspective, it is the broadband providers who hold the power to shape access to knowledge, ideas and beliefs – and, of course, to culture and entertainment. They control access to the Internet and the flow of traffic over the networks and therefore decide how that access should work, and they have the power to deny it. The cooperation agenda is about the entertainment industries targeting that structural power, demanding that the access be shaped to suit their commercial requirements. The entertainment industries came up with various forms that such 'cooperation' could take. Proposed measures included filtering all network traffic for files containing copyrighted content, or blocking a list of webpages deemed to contain infringing content. There was also the so-called 'three strikes' or graduated response, where the broadband providers could be asked to send warning notices and ultimately disconnect subscribers deemed by the rights-holders to have infringed. Overall, the cooperation agenda was about taking positive action against broadband subscribers who were alleged to have infringed copyright by downloading material over their Internet connection, as the following comment from an entertainment industry lobbying coalition indicates: 'Clear commitments from stakeholders, including in particular ISPs and other intermediaries, are needed to assist rights-holders in the fight against mass-scale online copyright theft.'[4]

The structural-power perspective explains why the entertainment industries targeted telecoms law in order to obtain that cooperation from the broadband providers. In the EU, they did this by drafting amendments to the 2009 Telecoms Package – a broad package of legal changes to the European telecoms framework. The following comment from the Motion Picture Association (MPA), representing the Hollywood studios, explains their viewpoint: 'it is both crucial and timely that the opportunity of the ongoing legislative review of the so-called Telecoms Package be seized to address this regulatory vacuum and to set the ground rules for stakeholder cooperation to be both encouraged and facilitated at the EU level.'[5]

It was a move that took the majority of policy observers by surprise, and many did not understand. Why would the entertainment industries target telecoms law? Copyright was outside the scope of the law and there would be no legal basis to include it. But it was precisely because the broadband providers had the power to determine the ways that content could be disseminated and accessed that the entertainment industries wanted to change the law that regulated those providers. This also explains why demands for 'cooperation' sparked an inter-industry political battle because the broadband providers did not readily agree, and they naturally positioned themselves to defend their power.

In the case of the 2009 EU Telecoms Package, the MPA and the IFPI led an entertainment industry-lobbying coalition calling itself the Creative and Media Business Alliance (CMBA).[6] The political context for this move was the 'three strikes' approach which had been taken up by the French government and was in the process of being written into French law. This was the Creation and Internet law[7] that formed the basis of the original 'three strikes and you're out' proposal, where users would be sent two warnings before being disconnected. The law was controversial, however, and had to be amended so that the disconnection notices were issued by a court and, in the end, only one subscriber was actually ever disconnected.[8] The entertainment industries wanted a similar approach to be Europe-wide, and so they sought to get provisions into the 2009 Telecoms Package that would support 'three strikes' measures. The CMBA tried to persuade the European Commission that: 'the French agreement is an interesting example with potential to be followed because it is founded on the idea that effective inter-industry cooperation is a key enabler [. . .] and all types of online violations of the law are fought jointly and efficiently'.[9]

They wanted the law to incorporate a requirement for Internet service providers to enforce copyright, built into the subscriber contracts, combined with powers for national regulators, such as Ofcom in Britain or the Arcep in France, to ask them to do so. Their thinking was to create a legal way to force broadband providers to take action on policing content. The aim was to facilitate suspension of subscriber accounts – or disconnection – in cases where the Internet access was used for downloading copyright files. In order to build that concept into telecoms law, they 'put forward concrete proposals for the Commission's consideration':[10] 'There should also be a general provision linking universal service obligations to a general requirement to respect the law. Suspension or termination for repeat infringement should also be treated within the framework.'[11]

The CMBA drafted two amendments to reflect their proposals.[12] What then happened was very strange indeed. Two remarkably similar amendments appeared without consultation in the Telecoms Package presented by the European Commission.[13] From what can be ascertained, these unexpected amendments had been put there against the wishes of the head of the telecoms unit, who had prepared the draft law.[14] Initially, they had the support of the Information Society Commissioner Viviane Reding, who specifically mentioned the inclusion of copyright when she presented

the Telecoms Package, on 13 November 2007, but who subsequently changed her mind as the law progressed through
the European Parliament. Rights-holder lobbyists praised the
amendments, pleased to see the recognition in the draft law
that 'network operators are involved in the means of distribution and access to content, among which is content protected
by droit d'auteur'.[15] These two amendments became known
as 'copyright hooks', but in fact neither of them survived.
One was deleted and not replaced, and the other, concerning
subscriber contracts, was redrafted within a broader-scoped
political compromise linked to a separate agenda on net
neutrality (see p. 107), such that Internet service providers would have to include any restrictions on Internet use
in their contracts with subscribers – those restrictions could
include copyright infringement but could also be for another
purpose.[16]

Nevertheless, it meant that copyright enforcement had got
on to the European telecoms agenda. It was the subject of a
raft of other amendments tabled during the first reading of
the 2009 Telecoms Package in the European Parliament.
These amendments directly reflected the entertainment
industry language of 'cooperation',[17] including an amendment that called on the telecom regulators to encourage
broadband providers to 'cooperate' with the entertainment
industries: *national regulatory authorities shall promote cooperation between undertakings providing electronic communications
services and the sectors interested in the protection and promotion
of lawful content*. Just as the CMBA had wanted to do, this
amendment would have given the national regulators a duty
to ask Internet service providers to police content on behalf of
rights-holders.[18]

This 'cooperation' amendment was traced back to a French
copyright-holders' organization, the Société des Auteurs et
Compositeurs Dramatiques (SACD), representing French
film directors. It was tabled an astonishing seven times, and
was found in four out of the five committee Opinions on the

Telecoms Package.[19] Interestingly, this was not a breach of process. Every proposed law will be the responsibility of a lead committee which will prepare a report for the Parliament to vote on, and other committees will submit their Opinions with amendments for consideration. This method of giving draft text to MEPs to table as amendments to Opinion committees is known by all lobbyists working in Brussels and sometimes it can be the route to getting amendments into European law, although it is unusual for them to be retabled to so many different committees.

The cooperation amendment was not adopted by the lead committee[20] since it did not have support from the lead rapporteur,[21] Catherine Trautmann, a French Socialist. After some crafty manoeuvres by MEPs on the 'right' of the European Parliament, who lent their support to the entertainment industries, a watered-down version of it was eventually adopted into law.[22] The final version removed the 'duty' on the regulators and introduced a weaker, optional possibility to establish 'talks' between the two industries,[23] and the result is that it has had very little effect. The important outcome of the Telecoms Package was agreed in a Third Reading in November 2009. The rapporteur, Catherine Trautmann, agreed a political compromise that reminded national governments of their duty to guarantee fundamental rights and, in particular, the right to due process. The provision – Article 1.3a of Directive 2009/140/EC – is sometimes referred to as the Internet Freedom Provision.[24] It states that any measures taken by governments to restrict the Internet, which also may restrict a person's fundamental rights, must guarantee a 'prior, fair and impartial procedure' for the person whose access or content is being restricted. The fundamental rights refer to the right to freedom of expression and the right to privacy. What it means is that governments who want to ask broadband providers to 'cooperate' with copyright-holders should ensure that anyone accused of infringement has a right to due process before the restriction is imposed. This principle here is that any decision to either block content or remove people's access to communications may be seen as an infringement of their right to freedom of expression, and therefore it must be done using due process. In simple terms, this means a court hearing. Article 1.3a highlighted a tension[25] between intellectual property rights[26] and the freedom of expression of Internet users.[27] This tension between different fundamental rights is broader in scope than just a commercial conflict, and that may be why it has subsequently proved difficult, if not impossible, to resolve copyright enforcement politically. There is a sense in which the right to freedom of expression acts as a bulwark against strong measures to protect intellectual property.

There was an unexpected addendum to the Telecoms Package, in the form of a commitment from the European Commission to run a consultation on net neutrality the following year.[28] The issue of net neutrality had become heated as it had become entangled with the copyright issue over the possibility of broadband providers implementing 'restrictions'. The final wording of the law had mandated providers to tell their subscribers about any 'conditions limiting access to and/or use of content, services and applications'[29] where a limiting condition could be blocking of infringing web-pages, or throttling the customers' Internet connection to prevent them from accessing peer-to-peer file-sharing services, or disconnection from the Internet. Hence, allowing broadband providers to apply restrictions, provided only that they tell their subscribers, would mitigate in favour of the entertainment industries and their political demands. Indeed, entertainment industry lobbyists, such as the French film industry organization Eurocinema, agreed that this language suited their requirements.[30]

The cooperation agenda therefore was also linked to the net-neutrality agenda, even though the two are sometimes incorrectly regarded as being quite separate. The large entertainment companies were simultaneously lobbying against net neutrality, for the same reason that they sought to amend telecoms law. They were advocating similar propositions to the US authorities as well as in the EU. For example, in its submission on net neutrality to the United States Federal Communications Commission (FCC), the Motion Picture Association of America (MPAA) demanded the use of network-based technology for copyright policing without a court order.[31] According to the MPAA, this would 'foster a flexible environment in which content owners and Internet service providers have the ability to develop and utilize the best available tools and technologies to combat the scourge of online content theft'. Since the use of such tools and technologies would interfere with the network traffic, the MPAA's position was incompatible with a net-neutrality principle.

The cooperation agenda again arose with regard to the Anti-Counterfeiting Trade Agreement (ACTA). This was a so-called free-trade agreement with the specific purpose of addressing intellectual property and copyright in international trade. Once again, the MPAA called for the broadband providers to assist with enforcing copyright, and this time the key expression was 'secondary liability', a legal term which, somewhat confusingly, is aimed at making a third party liable for a copyright infringement. Here is an example of how they advocated the idea to the United States Trade Representative:

> Practical secondary liability regimes for online infringement are essential to motivate participants to cooperate in implementing the reasonable practices that will make the online marketplace less hospitable for infringers. ACTA parties should refine their secondary liability regimes to reflect current realities and adopt modern, flexible systems where they do not exist. The goal must be to educate and encourage responsible conduct on the part of all parties involved in the transmission of copyright materials.[32]

The MPAA specifically called for Internet disconnection or graduated response measures to be included in the ACTA, and it called for a weakening of privacy law in order to facilitate the identification of infringing users, as in this example.

Note that the use of the word 'victim' is intended to mean the
MPAA members, who are the Hollywood studios:

> Overly strict interpretations of national data privacy rules
> increasingly impede enforcement against an array of wrongs
> that occur on the Internet, including copyright theft – often
> leaving victims without any means of redress. ACTA part-
> ners should ensure that the interpretation of data privacy
> rules appropriately balances the fundamental rights of pri-
> vacy and property, including intellectual property, in such
> a way as to encourage meaningful cooperation by telcos/
> ISPs, in particular the implementation of a legally acceptable
> 'graduated response' mechanism.[33]

The MPAA's strong influence over the US authorities is
likely to have led to US government negotiators seeking to
include broadband provider liability in the ACTA. But EU
law precluded its negotiators agreeing to those demands, and
ultimately the US had to back down.[34] However, the MPAA
example here does illustrate how the cooperation agenda also
hooks into the privacy agenda, and how it raises the other
aspect of structural power, namely, the power to protect or
threaten security. Privacy was an issue because the identity of
alleged infringers had to be known in order for them to be
disconnected. This information was known only to the broadband provider, who was bound by data-protection law not to
reveal it.

From the entertainment industry perspective, data-
protection law is a barrier to stronger copyright protection.
Surveillance conducted by the copyright-holders enabled
them to locate files downloaded by an individual user and the
Internet Protocol (IP) address allocated to them, but the law,
at least in the European Union, makes it difficult to obtain
personal contact data of the individual who was using that
IP address. The entertainment industries want to get hold of
identities and contact information of people whom they allege
to be infringing – hence, they demanded that broadband providers should release personal data of individuals alleged to be

sharing copyrighted content. They argued for weaker privacy law[35] to enable them to obtain personal details of individual users.

The tension between copyright and data protection was tested in the landmark case of *Promusicae* v. *Telefonica*.[36] Promusicae is an organization representing the Spanish recorded music industry. Telefonica is the largest telecoms provider in Spain. The Spanish music producers wanted to sue individual file-sharers who were exchanging music over the Internet. Using their own private surveillance techniques, they found out the IP addresses that were allocated to these individuals whilst conducting that activity but could not get names or addresses, which they would need in order to file a lawsuit. Those contact details were held by Telefonica. When Telefonica refused to hand them over, Promusicae went to court. Telefonica argued that it was not required to hand over the data because this was a civil-law case. Under Spanish law, only in criminal cases could the company be asked to supply third parties with personal data of its subscribers. The case went all the way to the European Court of Justice, which said that it was up to Spain (or any member-state government) to determine the balance between privacy rights and intellectual property rights. It ruled that European law did not preclude the state from ordering the data to be disclosed in civil cases, but also that the law did not require it. The ruling established the principle that where several fundamental rights are at stake, a 'fair balance' must be struck between the requirements of all.[37] In any event, the state should 'make sure that they do not rely on an interpretation of them which would be in conflict with those fundamental rights or with the other general principles of Community law, such as the principle of proportionality'.[38]

The cooperation agenda, therefore, seeks the weakening of net neutrality as well as privacy, in order to enable the entertainment industries to take advantage of the network providers' structural power and in turn to create new opportunities for stronger enforcement of copyright by means of blocking and restricting access to content.[39] Conversely, a strong net-neutrality principle, combined with tough privacy laws, would make certain enforcement measures regarding the Internet more difficult. Copyright-enforcement policy therefore sits on this pivot of privacy and net neutrality, and the outcome of all three policy debates will be critical in determining whether the Internet remains open or what level of restriction becomes acceptable.

CHAPTER EIGHT

Blocking Judgments

> This is an important case where one ISP stands alone
> before the court [but] there is no suggestion that the
> scale of the order will be limited to one ISP. It would
> wrong to see this as limited. If BT is asked to block,
> there will be more. At industry meetings BT has
> been told by rights-holders they would like 400 sites
> to be blocked. And it won't be limited to just
> copyright. I've been involved in cases where people
> complain about personal or defamatory information
> and ask us to block access to this or that blog. If this
> goes ahead, it will apply to all ISPs, and much more
> widely than just copyright.[1]

At the High Court in London, here was British Telecom's barrister warning of an increasing demand for Internet blocking
orders and reminding the court that any decision would have
far wider consequences than just the case in front of them.
BT had gone to court to try to get some red lines drawn as to
where the law stood on making network providers police content. The case set the precedent for a court order, and to some
extent limited the scope of what the network providers could
be asked to do. The underlying policy question is whether it is
appropriate that Internet industry – content platform or network – should act as policeman, judge and jury.

It's a complex issue that policymakers are struggling with.
In many ways, the law as it stands is silent. States increasingly
expect that the network providers and the content platforms
will take care of problems themselves. These corporations

have the power to shape the means of access knowledge. The content platforms, such as Google and its subsidiary YouTube, social media sites like Twitter and Facebook, online auction and shopping sites like eBay and Amazon, set the terms and the formats for users to upload content. The network providers – the likes of BT, Deutsche Telekom, France Telecom, Telefonica, Vodafone, AT&T and Verizon[2] – have automated management systems that can impose electronic content blocks. Where blocking orders are requested, these companies are being asked to use their power to deny access to information, culture or entertainment. This is the structural power in action.

Some activities take place over their infrastructure that are illegal or, if not illegal, then distasteful, offensive or socially unacceptable. There are commercial organizations and civil-society groups which believe that these activities should be policed, just as they would be in the physical world, and they argue that the best way to deal with such content is to remove it or block it. However, in many instances, it is not always a black-and-white issue that the content should be removed. Sometimes there is a fine line between the legal and the illegal, and intermediaries are effectively being asked to make an ethical and legal judgment. Examples that fall into this 'grey' area include graphic violence, sexual images or defamatory speech, and also copyright.

Graphic violence, for example, has presented a particularly difficult challenge. In the evolving international political context, videos have been posted on the large content platforms showing scenes from war and conflict situations; for example, some very brutal footage has been posted from the Syrian conflict. There is an issue concerning how deletion requests should be balanced against the public interest. For example, is it possible to differentiate between footage designed to publicize brutality or incite violent conflict versus footage uploaded by a citizen-journalist to inform the rest of the world about politically motivated violence, where there may be good reasons for that content to remain online? This raises another challenge, namely, terrorism and what are often termed 'extremist' views, notably content that incites acts of terrorism or in some other way presents a threat to national security. The head of the British intelligence agency GCHQ, Robert Hannigan, writing in the *Financial Times*, argued that the US-owned content platforms and social media networks had 'become the command and control networks of choice for terrorists, who find their services as transformational as the rest of us'.[3] Mr Hannigan accused the content platforms of being 'in denial' about the way their systems are being used and called on them to take action. Government sources indicated that the initial policy response was to demand the automated removal or filtering of such content, as in this extract from the minutes of a meeting:

> [. . .] James Brokenshire met with the four ISPs to talk about the inclusion of extremist material in their family friendly filters. The Minister is hugely grateful to ISPs, and is clear there is shared responsibility here, with lots of different pieces to the jigsaw. [. . .]Filtering often doesn't reach content on social media platforms. The HO is in conversation with major social media companies about 'safe mode' – have spoken to Google, Facebook etc.[4]

This is therefore an issue of structural power that is perceived on the one hand to be obstructive by not 'taking responsibility' and on the other hand is perceived to have the ability to place restrictions by blocking unreasonably or illegally, and violating free-speech rights.

In fact, Google and Facebook would say that they do take some responsibility for what happens on their platforms.[5] They have put in place policies and processes for dealing with content-removal requests in a manner which they would say is ethical. That does not mean that all governments will agree with it. From their perspective, their challenge is how to deal with requests to suppress content without putting the entire platform at risk of losing users. It is a delicate balance between preserving the ability for people to be informed while avoiding the situation where their service turns into a propaganda or 'state-approved' platform. Their policies are developed internally but also discussed with advocacy groups and governments. These policies have to be explicable across many different cultures. They say that they work with law-enforcement authorities, but requests, warrants and orders from any government are scrutinized by their internal compliance departments before taking the decision whether to assist.

One implication for Internet users is that the legality of a request for content to be taken down is being determined or judged by someone in a different jurisdiction. In many cases, corporate staff at Google or Facebook will be deciding whether or not content is unacceptable, and it begs the question whether they are making a determination about what is and is not free speech. Google and Facebook argue that they are being as transparent as they can be, by publishing data regarding the numbers of take-down requests, including those from law enforcement, on a worldwide basis. Other content platforms such as Twitter have begun to follow suit, as have some network providers such as Vodafone.

The issue is that here are private corporations making these determinations across all jurisdictions, and it is arguable that they are taking on a quasi-judicial role on a global basis. In setting internal 'policies', one might suggest that they are also setting de facto international laws and potentially bypassing the sovereignty of national governments. This embeds their structural power, especially if national governments seek to rely on them for content removal. Unsurprisingly, they argue for the continuance of this system and against any kind of state intervention. Imposing new rules on them, they say, would ultimately have the effect of silencing minorities, and that is a difficult logic for a democratic government to argue against.

Copyrights and wrongs

The issue of policing content has been tested the most in the context of copyright enforcement, and there is a sense in which copyright has led the way towards blocking injunctions. Copyright enforcement presents a conflict between two knowledge structures. The entertainment corporations were seeking to defend their existing structures designed for the analogue era, and the Internet industries were resisting demands to alter their structures for the benefit of what would have been seen as an old business model. It is the cooperation agenda again, with a different twist. As outlined in chapter 7, the entertainment industries have lobbied for legal changes in telecoms law, to support their case. Having failed to get all the changes they wanted, the entertainment industries have tried other routes, including the courts. What is often not understood is how the court actions are connected to the higher-level political agenda.

Google, and increasingly Facebook and other content platforms, receive a high volume of copyright take-down requests and, in this context, they perform a quasi-judicial role. A take-down request is a request to remove content from the platform, so it would no longer exist. In the United States, the process for take-down requests is established in law. This is the Digital Millennium Copyright Act (DMCA),[6] which established a balance between the ability of the content platform to distribute content, and the rights of the entertainment industries to protect their copyright. It did so by means of a legal 'safe harbor' for intermediaries. 'Safe harbor' gave them immunity from liability if they were merely storage or search facilities, had no knowledge of the infringing content, did not benefit financially from it and acted promptly to take down content when made aware of it. There was a possibility for the person who uploaded the content to make a counterclaim. The content platforms were not expected to seek out content that they did not know about, and provided they acted in accordance with the law when informed about infringing content, they could not be sued for damages. In this way, it was argued that the law recognized that content platforms could not build a business if they faced unlimited liability claims from copyright-holders.

This system is known as 'notice and take-down'. It is now beginning to sink under the weight of requests. In 2013, Google received an astonishing 235 *million* take-down requests for copyright-infringing links to be taken out of its search-engine results. This was an exponential rise from the 10 million received in 2011 and it continued to increase. By 2015, Google was receiving requests at the rate of 35.5 million per month and a quick calculation indicates that this is double the 2013 volume.[7] Most of those requests were identified and filed by means of automated systems that cannot distinguish between content that is lawful or unlawful. In an attempt to find an appropriate balance, Google implemented a practice of checking the alleged infringing URLs and forming its own decision whether to remove them or let them remain. It has been calculated that in 2013 Google discarded around 9 per cent – or 21 *million* – of the take-down requests for search-engine link removal, including inaccurate filings and duplicates.[8]

Lawfulness could be established under the US 'fair-use' defence. The seminal case was *Stephanie Lenz* v. *Universal Music*,[9] in 2008, where a mother who had posted a video of her children dancing to a track by the singer Prince was hit with a take-down request from Universal Music. She had issued a counter-notice, claiming fair use under US copyright law, and YouTube had subsequently reinstated it. The ruling confirmed that the take-down notice had been improperly issued, and established that the possibility of a fair-use defence should be considered before requesting removal of material with a take-down notice.[10] Another example of a fair-use challenge occurred in a case brought by the famous copyright scholar, Lawrence Lessig, who successfully challenged a music company over an automated removal of his video from YouTube.[11] The video contained snippets of a song, and Lessig claimed his right to use them under the fair-use principle.

Google's determinations are made under US law. European law was written after the DMCA and, although it offers a form of immunity for content platforms in Article 14 of the E-commerce Directive,[12] it is not exactly the same. There is no formal structure for a notice and take-down system, and, where US law does apply to search engines, there is a question mark over EU law on this point.[13] A proposal for a new European directive to put in place such a system was the subject of political controversy and was shelved. Specifically, the entertainment industry lobbyists objected to a proposal for a counter-notice.[14]

The entertainment industries have tried to sue Google. A landmark case was *Viacom* v. *YouTube*, launched in 2008 by a group of US entertainment companies, alleging massive copyright infringement against YouTube and seeking up to $1 billion in damages.[15] Essentially, Viacom, having filed 100,000 take-down requests, claimed that YouTube was 'inducing' infringements and as a consequence did not qualify for DMCA 'safe harbor' protection. It was trying to establish a case of secondary liability for those infringements. Viacom did not succeed. Three separate judgments in 2010,[16] 2012 and 2013[17] ruled in favour of YouTube. It was clear from then on that YouTube did qualify for 'safe harbor' protection. Analysis of the case by the Electronic Frontier Foundation (EFF) argued that Viacom appeared to be asking for a broad reinterpretation of the DMCA. The EFF suggested that Viacom was probing the DMCA to try to establish a case of secondary liability, in order to sue other content platforms for financial damages. However, it is too easy to view the Viacom case as just a technical legal argument over a liability. It is one of the landmark court battles between the old and new media, where old media seeks to use its financial muscle to wipe out a new, innovative competitor. It had not banked on the new competitor having a strong legal budget. If Viacom had succeeded, said the EFF, the effect would have been to hobble innovation, with serious consequences not only for YouTube, but also for Twitter and Flickr and many innovations yet to come.

YouTube's legal victory over Viacom may have created a barrier for other entertainment companies to sue, and they have since tried other methods of pressuring Google. For example, in 2013, the British Phonographic Industries (BPI) began filing a million take-down requests per week to Google.[18] They argued that Google could not possibly be ignorant of the fact that some of the websites concerned were infringing copyright, and they wanted Google to take a higher-level action against them, as illustrated by the following quote from BPI chief executive Geoff Taylor:

> I don't think it's enough for Google to sit back and say, tell me each illegal file one by one and we'll remove the results. If Google is clever enough to teach a computer to think – even if only about cats – it's clever enough, when it has been told more than 150,000 times that The Pirate Bay is illegal, to rank that site below Amazon and iTunes when consumers search for music.[19]

The Pirate Bay was the key target of the entertainment industries in Europe. It enabled individuals to share music and film files with each other. Technically, it was a BitTorrent tracker, meaning that it used a protocol known as BitTorrent, and only stored files which contained information about the content, but not the content itself: the files containing the content were stored on the users' own computers. The BitTorrent technology enabled users to download from multiple computers at any one time, meaning that it could work particularly fast (and this is part of the reason for its popularity). The evidence against The Pirate Bay had been gathered in for several years. It was the largest file-sharing site worldwide, although exact figures for its traffic are a little hard to establish. From what can be ascertained, in 2006 it had around 700,000 registered users and in 2008 it had 20 million users and was in the top 100 websites. The user base grew to 30 million in 2012 and more than 50 million in 2014.[20] Following a police raid in 2006,[21] a case for criminal complicity in breach of the Swedish Copyright Act was heard in the Stockholm District Court.[22] The ruling, released in 2009, found that The Pirate Bay owners had 'facilitated and, consequently, aided and abetted these offences'. In other words, they were found guilty of a form of secondary liability,[23] despite the fact that the court acknowledged that they had not had any direct input into the choice of content, and that the site would qualify as a host under Article 14 of the European Commerce Directive.

The case against The Pirate Bay was led by the recorded music industry and the Hollywood movie studios[24] amid allegations that the case was politically motivated.[25] Correspondence between the MPAA and the Swedish authorities from 2006 suggested there had been pressure from the US government. This extract is from a letter allegedly sent to the Swedish Justice Minister:

> As I am sure you are aware, the American Embassy has sent entreaties to the Swedish government urging it to take action against The Pirate Bay and other organizations operating within Sweden that facilitate copyright theft. As we discussed during our meeting, it is certainly not in Sweden's best interests to earn a reputation among other nations and trading partners as a place where utter lawlessness with respect to intellectual property is tolerated. I would urge you once again to exercise your influence to urge law enforcement authorities in Sweden to take much-needed action against The Pirate Bay.[26]

From a structural-power perspective, it may be possible to make an argument that The Pirate Bay and other BitTorrent sites represented a new type of structure and so they became a target of the entertainment industries. The Pirate Bay is interesting because it proved to be a pivotal case in Europe, prompting several follow-up cases against network providers for Internet blocking orders against The Pirate Bay and other file-sharing sites. The entertainment industries argued that the broadband providers were liable for copyright infringement because they were permitting the infringing activity on their networks, and they relied on a provision in the EU Copyright Directive[27] that enabled them to bring an injunction against intermediaries. In 2008, a case filed by IFPI, in Denmark, resulted in a blocking order against the Internet service provider Tele2.[28] The ruling was upheld in a high-court appeal in November 2008, but was further appealed in the Danish Supreme Court with the support of the Danish telecommunications industry association. There was concern from Danish telecoms industry about the possibility of setting a legal precedent. However, they lost the appeal in 2012.[29] There was a similar filing in Italy by an IFPI-affiliated anti-piracy organization. The blocking order was handed down on 8 August 2008 by a court in the city of Bergamo, in the north of Italy. Italian Internet users who attempted to access The Pirate Bay were redirected to a police notice, telling them that access was blocked, although the decision was reversed on appeal.

From 2012, the entertainment industries began filing for blocking orders in the UK,[30] after it became obvious that the law they had lobbied for – the Digital Economy Act – would be delayed in its implementation, if it ever happened at all. They sought blocking injunctions under Section 97a of the UK's Copyright, Designs and Patents Act (CDPA) (the UK implementation of the EU Copyright Directive, Section 8.3).[31] The outcomes of these cases have established some red lines for blocking orders, and they have also highlighted some problems that may arise when network providers are asked to police content.

The first blocking orders concerned a site known as Newzbin. The Pirate Bay orders came subsequently. However, the two Newzbin cases set the parameters for those subsequent orders. Importantly, the judge in the first Newzbin case refused to grant an order for an entire site to be blocked.

Instead, he limited the blocking to the repertoire of the claimant companies only. His reasoning was that the site as a whole
might contain non-copyrighted material belonging to other
individuals, and therefore an injunction against the entire site
would pose legal uncertainties:

> [T]he claimants are seeking an injunction to restrain activi-
> ties in relation to all binary and all text materials in respect
> of which they own no rights and about which I have heard
> little or no evidence [. . .] the rights of all other rights hold-
> ers are wholly undefined and consequently the scope of
> the injunction would be very uncertain. In my judgment the
> scope of any injunction under section 97A(2) should extend
> no further than that to which I have already concluded the
> claimants are entitled, namely an injunction to restrain
> the defendant from infringing the claimants' copyrights in
> relation to their repertoire.[32]

In the second Newzbin case, *Twentieth Century Fox* v.
British Telecom (BT),[33] this limitation of scope was pursued
by BT, who asked the court for an order with a list of specific
webpages or addresses.[34] BT specifically argued against blocking an entire website on the basis that it was tantamount to
an imposition of a general monitoring requirement under
the E-commerce Directive.[35] In order to implement such
a block, BT argued that it would have to identify and intercept all traffic on its network that was heading towards the
Newzbin site. Hence, this would put it in breach of EU law.
However, BT's argument was not accepted. The ruling instead
accepted the entertainment-industry argument that BT had
already implemented network-level blocking technology for a
different purpose, and the order would not impose excessive
costs.[36] Therefore BT's request was not granted. The ruling
additionally stated that an interference with the rights of any
non-infringing content was *de minimis*.[37] However, the case
did establish the precedent that entertainment industries
wishing to ask network providers to block copyrighted content must first of all obtain a court order, and that was an

important red line in the law. *Twentieth Century Fox* v. *BT* was followed by a raft of claims for blocking of The Pirate Bay. For example, in *Dramatico Entertainment* v. *BskyB*,[38] the British music industry took action against six of the network providers, including mobile networks. The defendants were the six largest British Internet service providers, BSkyB, BT, Everything Everywhere, TalkTalk, Telefonica and Virgin Media, but they did not turn up in court to defend their position. The point of the case was simply to get the court order. What was interesting in this case is that it was a judgment on The Pirate Bay itself, despite the fact that The Pirate Bay did not have any servers in Britain, and its proprietors were not in court.[39] The ruling asserted that British users of The Pirate Bay were infringing copyright by both copying and by communicating the works to the public.[40] It further stated that The Pirate Bay 'is in no sense a passive repository', having failed to take down files that had been notified as infringing.[41] Hence, the court applied a notion of secondary liability similar in its language to Swedish ruling and concluded:

> that the operators of TPB induce, incite or persuade its users to commit infringements of copyright, and that they and the users act pursuant to a common design to infringe. It is also relevant in this regard that the operators profit from their activities. Thus they are jointly liable for the infringements committed by users.[. . .] For the reasons set out above, I conclude that both users and the operators of TPB infringe the copyrights of the Claimants (and those they represent) in the UK.

The *Dramatico* ruling relied on evidence from an anti-piracy expert, stating that there were approximately 1 million Torrent files hosted on The Pirate Bay in 2011, of which 750,000 were commercially available.[42] The assumption made was that these were all infringing files, but what would the situation have been if some of these were not infringing – for example, files uploaded by musicians of their own music? This raises one of the complexities of blocking orders, where legitimate

content is caught up in a block ordered for something unconnected to it. This is known as over-blocking and it did occur
as the unintended consequence of another British copyright
blocking order. The Premier League had sued BSkyB, and
obtained a court order for the network operator to block an
unlicensed website that was streaming football games. The
order mandated that an Internet Protocol (IP) address should
be blocked, relying on evidence from the Premier League
that IP address-blocking would be specific to the target site
and would not block any other content, 'since that IP address
is not shared'.[43] However, the IP address being blocked was,
in fact, used for redirection and was shared by multiple sites.
BSkyB's implementation of the order had managed to block
the *Radio Times* – a listings site published by the BBC – which
is, of course, legal content.[44] The editor of the *Radio Times*
made his feelings clear in this quote to the *Financial Times*:

> It's outrageous that our website has been suddenly switched
> off and our users wrongly informed that it's to protect against
> copyright infringement.[. . .] The Premier League seems to
> be behaving like the worst sort of blundering striker who's
> forgotten the first rule of football – check you're at the right
> end before you shoot.[45]

Over-blocking is possible in any situation where an automated block is placed on Internet content and, as illustrated
by the *Radio Times* example, it raises problems concerning
the violation of free speech. The matter was addressed by
the European Court of Human Rights (EctHR) in the case
of *Yildirim* v. *Turkey*,[46] where an entirely legal website hosted
on Google's cloud-based service (then known as GoogleSites)
had been caught in a block placed on another site that was
subject to criminal proceedings. The EctHR found in favour
of the claimant, Yildirim, establishing that his right to freedom of expression had been violated by the blocking order.

In general, blocking orders engage the right to freedom of
expression under Article 10 of the European Convention on
Human Rights (ECHR). This means that the right to freedom

of expression must be taken into account, and balanced against any competing rights – copyright would count as a competing right. Article 10 states that the right to freedom of expression must be guaranteed *without interference* from a public authority and, on the Internet, blocking is considered to be interference. The right to freedom of expression applies to transmission of data over the network, not just to the content, and it applies even where there is profit-making involved, as there could be in a copyright-infringement case. However, the state does have the right to restrict freedom of expression if it is deemed 'necessary in a democratic society'.[47] This means that governments or courts may order blocking of content, for copyright infringement or any other reason, but the order must be justified by its necessity and proportionality. These are legal terms which are subject to interpretation, but are an attempt to create a balance between a genuine need to remove content for society's protection on the one hand, and biased, arbitrary or politically motivated blocks on the other.

The Court of Human Rights has established key criteria for Internet blocking orders. The criteria include clear definitions of the type of person who could have their content blocked, the type of blocking mechanism, a time limit to be imposed, the interests that will be served by the order, notification to the person affected, a clear process for implementation and the possibility of judicial appeal. Orders must also comply with the legal principles of proportionality and necessity. Blocking measures that interfere with lawful content are not legal, and nor are orders that remain valid indefinitely.[48]

In the absence of any policy direction at either EU or national level, there remain some critical issues related to blocking orders and free speech and, for this reason, blocking measures should only be carried out when strictly necessary and on the basis of a law, with judicial oversight in place. It is clear that the barracking for technology companies to 'take responsibility' is very much a double-edged sword. The delegation of regulatory responsibility to the large content platforms is arguably an obfuscation of government duty, which reflects a failure in policymaking and does urgently need to be addressed. Do we really want Google and Facebook to act as quasi-judicial regulators, and whose law will they be applying? Moreover, how much would this increase their structural power next time they need something from the state?

CHAPTER NINE

A Dark Cloud

> Today the online market has further fragmented and
> content thieves are taking advantage of new online
> technologies, with streaming sites and cyberlockers
> representing a growing share of unlawful conduct.[1]

This quote, from a Motion Picture Association of America
(MPAA) submission in 2010 to United States trade-policy
officials, suggests that 'cyberlockers' were being targeted
over copyright infringement. 'Cyberlocker' is an alternative,
and somewhat outmoded, term for a cloud-storage service –
remotely located services that enable people to upload their
photos, documents, movies, music or business data and
access their own files over the Internet from anywhere they
happen to be. According to the MPAA, which represents the
major Hollywood studios,[2] these services were being used to
distribute copyright-infringing files on a grand scale, hence it
was raising its concern. That's one perspective.

To take a different perspective, there is a whole new industry
forming around 'cloud services', which is supported by some
very large technology corporations such as Microsoft. It's an
industry that governments want to encourage, and one that
is central to the European Union's new Digital Single Market
strategy. The benefit of cloud services is that people don't have
to carry the material everywhere with them, but would always
be able to access it; the services are widely used for streaming audio-visual files, but this is only one of the many possible
uses. Cloud services are new structures in the Internet ecosystem, and these new structures have the ability to control

the storage and retrieval of knowledge and information, hence they have the potential to achieve structural power.

With those two perspectives in mind, the shutdown of the cloud-based service Megaupload by the United States authorities highlights a deeply divisive controversy and, at the time of going to press, it was stuck in the middle of a legal battle in the New Zealand courts,[3] without a resolution. Megaupload was a cloud service with more than 60 million registered users, and 1 billion unique visitors per year, making it the market leader for this kind of service in 2011–12.[4] The service was shut down in January 2012, in an internationally coordinated action, orchestrated by the Federal Bureau of Investigation (FBI). It entailed a James Bond-style special forces police helicopter raid on a private mansion in New Zealand, and the arrest at gunpoint of Megaupload's proprietor, a larger-than-life German businessman known as Kim Dotcom.[5] Simultaneously, the domain name was seized and the service taken offline.[6] To some observers, this would seem to be a heavy-handed reaction for a case of alleged copyright piracy. It was described as a mega failure for the cloud-computing industry[7] because it highlighted a business risk, namely, that providers living under threat of closure by governments or third parties could not offer long-term data security. Concern was expressed that the site also hosted many personal files, raising free-speech issues, and that this would not be the last of this type of shutdown.[8]

The closure of Megaupload occurred in a political context where the entertainment industries, notably the MPAA, were lobbying the US government to do something about what they called 'rogue foreign sites' – websites operating outside the US which offered infringing content. Megaupload appears to have been put into this category because it was operated by a Hong Kong registered company and had servers in the Netherlands as well as the US.[9] In November 2010,[10] and again in October 2011,[11] in letters to the United States Trade Representative (USTR), the MPAA alleged that Megaupload was 'driven by the vast amounts of infringing premium content available to users', although this allegation has never been proved.

'Foreign-based and foreign-controlled websites' became the object of a new, dedicated task force on intellectual property, established by the Obama administration to coordinate efforts internally within the US Department of Justice. This new task force was called the National Intellectual Property Rights Coordination Center, in Arlington, Virginia. Its role was to work with the FBI, Immigration and Customs Enforcement (ICE), and other US government agencies.[12] Foreign websites were deemed to be 'a growing problem that undermines national security, particularly national economic security'. According to this quote from the US government's strategy document, federal agencies were asked to work with foreign governments and with the private sector on this specific issue:

> Despite the scope and increasing prevalence of such sites, enforcement is complicated because of the limits of the U.S. Government's jurisdiction and resources in foreign countries. To help better address these enforcement issues, federal agencies [. . .] will expeditiously assess current efforts to combat such sites and will develop a coordinated and comprehensive plan to address them that includes: (1) U.S. law enforcement agencies vigorously enforcing intellectual property laws; (2) U.S. diplomatic and economic agencies working with foreign governments and international organizations; and (3) the U.S. Government working with the private sector.[13]

The story of the Megaupload closure began in the summer of 2009, where, at the National Intellectual Property Rights Coordination Center, a special agent,[14] seconded from Immigration and Customs Enforcement (ICE), was following up a referral on an alleged copyright offence. From what can be ascertained, the referral came from the MPAA.[15] It concerned an operation known as Ninja Video,[16] which was put under investigation for criminal copyright infringement.

The special agent identified Ninja Video on servers run by Megaupload, and located in a Virginia data centre operated by a company called Carpathia Hosting. On 24 June 2010, almost a year after the investigation had begun, ICE obtained a search-and-seizure warrant regarding Ninja Video from the District Court for the Eastern District of Virginia.[17] Among the items to be seized was the content stored on Megaupload servers.[18]

Megaupload's defence attorneys claim that the site operators had been asked to leave the infringing Ninja Video content in place, pending further instruction.[19] They claimed that Megaupload cooperated with this request. They further claim that it cooperated with other notice and take-down[20] requests from copyright owners, and had even offered them a 'backdoor' to its site so that they could take down content themselves. Megaupload's owner, Kim Dotcom, has subsequently stated that he had legal advice to the effect that complying with the DMCA would protect him from legal action by copyright owners.[21]

However, Megaupload was not aware that it was itself the target of an investigation which appears to have commenced in March 2010[22] and was carried out by the FBI over many months, during which its agents obtained email correspondence with subscribers, advertisers and service providers, and even bank details.[23] In January 2012, a grand jury indictment was issued in the Eastern Virginia District Court.[24] A grand jury's role is to investigate cases to assess their merit for prosecution. The indictment contained allegations of 'a worldwide criminal organisation known as the "Mega Conspiracy" said to be an internationally organized criminal enterprise, responsible for criminal infringement of copyrighted works for private financial gain'[25] and which had caused 'harm to copyright holders well in excess of $500 million'. These are substantially serious allegations that Kim Dotcom and his colleagues have denied. It was alleged – and denied by Mr Dotcom – that Megaupload had encouraged the dissemination of infringing links in order to boost advertising revenues, and was criminally responsible for the actions of its users – a form of secondary liability. The indictment stated thirteen charges including conspiracy to commit copyright infringement, conspiracy to commit racketeering, conspiracy to commit money laundering, criminal copyright infringement by aiding and abetting, and fraud. Kim Dotcom consistently denied all the charges. Speaking to the New Zealand television network in March 2012, he said, 'I am not a copyright pirate'.[26] At the time of going to press, Mr Dotcom was in the New Zealand courts, fighting his extradition to the US. The case regarding the specific allegations of copyright infringement had yet to be heard.[27]

Mr Dotcom's lawyers have described the case as 'an alarming precedent for regulation of the Internet, freedom of expression, privacy rights, and the very rule of law' and, citing the huge volume of non-infringing, non-copyrighted material that resided on the servers, they alleged a violation of the fundamental rights of Megaupload users.[28] In a document issued publicly on their website in 2013, they argued that the US courts did not have jurisdiction over Megaupload since its management and staff were residents of New Zealand and not US citizens.[29] They further argued that there is no criminal liability for secondary copyright infringement under US law, and they claimed that Megaupload had understood that it was complying with US copyright law as stated in this extract:

> Megaupload was in the process of cooperating with a U.S. government investigation into alleged infringement by a third-party user of the service. Megaupload purposefully left intact certain infringing movies identified to it by the government, in order to preserve the status quo and the integrity of the FBI's investigation. Subsequently, in its applications for search warrants to seize the company's domain names, the government would tell the federal court that the company had been told about those infringing movies, but had failed to take them down, omitting the fact that Megaupload did so in order to cooperate with the ongoing investigation.[30]

Further to that, Mr Dotcom's New Zealand barrister had argued that the case against him was strongly contested, as per this extract from a 2013 court judgment:

> For Mr Dotcom, Mr Davison QC noted that the United States' case is based on its interpretation of Megaupload's business model: the reward programme, the abuse tool and so on. He said that Mr Dotcom wished to challenge the United States' interpretation of the business model at the extradition hearing in order to demonstrate that the inferences that the United States seeks to draw are unfounded.[31]

However, it was the dramatic dawn raid on Kim Dotcom's home near Auckland, New Zealand, that caught the public imagination. The raid was done through the cooperation of American and New Zealand law-enforcement authorities. The FBI's role in directing the raid can be validated from court documents,[32] as can the role of the New Zealand elite Special Tactics Group (STG). Video footage from closed-circuit television cameras was shown in the New Zealand court (and later webcast by New Zealand television channel 3 News).[33] It was eye-opening. The time was 6.45 a.m. on 20 January 2012. The camera was inside the police helicopter as it edged downwards towards the sleeping mansion in the countryside near Auckland that was Mr Dotcom's home. As the helicopter hovered just above the sweeping driveway inside the security gates, four men from New Zealand's elite Special Tactics Group sprang out and ran towards the building. Four police vans appeared at the back entrance and more officers jumped out, running. One of the vans contained police dogs. According to the STG officer who gave evidence in court in August 2012, FBI officers were there too and the 'primary objective was to secure the suspect to prevent him from destroying evidence'.

Speaking in the New Zealand courtroom in 2012, Kim Dotcom said he was woken up early in the morning by the sound of a helicopter circling above. He heard shouts and banging. He pressed a panic alarm to alert his security guards, before getting out of bed and going into a strong room that had been built into the top of the house. In his account, given to the court, he left the door of the strong room open so that the police offices could walk right in. He did not wait outside the room since he felt it might give them a shock 'to see me popping out',[34] and preferred to wait inside with his hands up, which is what he did, until the police officers entered the room. His security guards were made to wait outside in the courtyard, with his pregnant wife, Mona, their children and their nannies. Simultaneously, the FBI had raided the servers in Virginia, and seized Megaupload's domains, and the site disappeared from the Internet. On the day of the raid, the MPAA issued a press release, applauding the role of the US authorities in conducting it:[35]

> This criminal case, more than two years in development, shows that law enforcement can take strong action to protect American intellectual property stolen through sites housed in the United States. Similar tools are needed to go after foreign-based websites that threaten the livelihoods of the 2.2 million hardworking Americans whose jobs depend on the motion picture and television industry.[36]

Following the raid, and arrest of Mr Dotcom and his colleagues, a bitter and protracted court battle commenced. It was tough and heavily contested on both sides.

There have been several court hearings in New Zealand, and the court papers have been used in order to develop this account of the Megaupload story. The New Zealand courts did not rule on the merits of the US government's allegations, but they did address two separate issues. Firstly, there was the demand for Mr Dotcom's extradition to the United States, and his fight for disclosure of the US government's evidence against him. Secondly, there was the validity of the search warrants for the raid on his home and seizure of his property. In 2012, Kim Dotcom had challenged the validity of the search warrants,[37] and initially won a ruling in his favour in the New Zealand High Court. He fought against his extradition and was initially successful in delaying it. The case was postponed multiple times. It finally came to court in Auckland, New Zealand, on 21 September 2015.[38] He is said to have spent around 10 million New Zealand dollars on his defence and sold shares in his new company to raise money.[39] The matter was ongoing at the time of going to press.[40]

In 2014, the MPAA and the Recording Industry Association of America (RIAA) both filed civil-law suits against Megaupload for copyright infringement, calling for the freezing of his assets and demanding damages of $US100 million. In 2015, Mr Dotcom's personal financial assets were seized by the US authorities, who obtained a civil-forfeiture ruling in 2015, but it was subsequently declared invalid by the New Zealand courts because it had been ordered by default, in other words, without the presence of the defendant.[41] At the time of going to press, the RIAA civil suit had been delayed by order of a Virginia court.[42]

From the viewpoint of an innovative, start-up cloud-services company, this kind of treatment at the hands of government authorities is daunting, and poses quite serious business risks. A cloud service is entrusted with the files of many people. Users who had stored their files on the Megaupload servers had been denied access to their own material from the date of the raid on 19 January 2012. In some cases, they lost business files and others lost personal items such as photos. A separate legal case was filed in the United States by the Electronic Frontier Foundation (EFF), challenging the US government for its actions and inaction in the Megaupload case. The EFF asserted that Kyle Goodwin, the user whom it represented, had signed a standard cloud-computing contract[43] but was now facing the loss of rights to his own property, due to the over-broad nature of the order by the US authorities. The EFF further asserted that the US authorities had conducted a search of Mr Goodwin's files found on the Megaupload server. The EFF opened the claim, saying: 'It is one thing to take legal action against an alleged copyright infringer. It is quite another to do so at the expense of entirely innocent third parties, with no attempt to prevent or even mitigate the collateral damage.'[44]

In the background to this case is the possibility that it was motivated by corporate interests. Kim Dotcom, speaking in an interview with the website TorrentFreak, alleged that the MPAA were behind the raid.[45] The allegation was denied by the US Attorney General, Eric Holder,[46] and by the MPAA.[47]

It is a matter of record that there was a close relationship between the Democrats and the MPAA, going back many years. The US Vice President Joe Biden has been described as a strong advocate for intellectual property rights,[48] and in 2009 he was a guest speaker at a plush MPAA dinner.[49] MPAA donations to the Democrats are a matter of public record, and this may be an indicator of their political pulling power. Data analysis by the Sunlight Foundation, which investigates lobbying and political donations in the US, suggests that a substantial share (62 per cent) of MPAA political donations went to the Democrats.[50] Of course, it is unclear how much influence, if any, this might have achieved, but MPAA chairman Chris Dodd, in a Fox television interview, famously reminded the Democrats how much they owed his organization:[51]

> Candidly, those who count on quote 'Hollywood' for support need to understand that this industry is watching very carefully who's going to stand up for them when their job is at stake ... Don't ask me to write a check for you when you think your job is at risk and then don't pay any attention to me when my job is at stake.[52]

Mr Dodd's outburst occurred just before a Senate vote on the Stop Online Piracy Act (SOPA), a bill that the MPAA had been lobbying for. SOPA would have legitimized the targeting of foreign rogue websites – as discussed above, Megaupload would have fallen into that category.

The MPAA has named, in its own disclosures, the government departments it had visited with regard to Internet-related copyright enforcement. In the second quarter of 2010, the MPAA held meetings with the Department of Justice and with ICE. Through 2010–11, it declared meetings with the FBI, Homeland Security and Justice departments on topics including 'rogue piracy sites legislation' and 'digital piracy DHS/ICE enforcement efforts'.[53] In the third quarter of 2010, it spent $520,000 on lobbying in Washington, and in the last quarter of 2011, its expenditure went up to $850,000, coinciding with the two copyright enforcement bills being processed in Congress (SOPA and Protect IP Act or PIPA), and the run-up to the raid on Megaupload. Nevertheless, the publicly available evidence is very much circumstantial and the true nature of the MPAA's influence may well be buried in piles of emails in a Justice Department office.

The Megaupload case signals how closely states and private corporations may work together for a perceived common interest. The wider policy issue concerns the future for cloud services. A decision taken over a single content issue, such as copyright, may have much wider implications for other policy goals. Cloud services are developing new structures for information distribution and attracting millions of users, but their business depends on gaining the trust of their users. So was this the structural-power argument in reverse? These were emerging structures over which the entertainment industries have no control, but in their emergent state, they also had no political power. Were they targeted on the assumption that they had no power and possibly no resources to fight back? Until cloud-services companies become sufficiently large and financially wealthy to obtain political influence, they will be vulnerable. Their vulnerability is multifold, due to the many different interests which want to block access to content, and which also may want access to their data for surveillance or profiling purposes.

CHAPTER TEN

Closing Pressures

Does politics shape the Internet or does the Internet shape politics? The vision of corporate lobbyists advocating in Brussels and Washington would suggest the former. The notion of the below-the-waterline network infrastructure suggests the latter. The possibilities for telecoms companies to manipulate their networks, restricting access to content by means of altering the physical routing of information, implies a sovereignty that many liberal-democratic governments would envy. Likewise, the ability of the large content platforms to use data profiles and shape the content preferences for some 1.7 billion users worldwide implies an intimidating political supremacy.

The notion of structural power has been there right through this book because it seems to fit hand-in-glove with the Internet. Network providers and content platforms do have the power to shape access to knowledge, ideas and beliefs by means of their control of the networks and the arrangements to deliver content. They also have the power to threaten our security by means of the possibilities for intrusion on our privacy through the use, private trading or handing over to the authorities of personal data. The cases in this book have illustrated how they use that power to shape political agendas.

Structural power is not an overt power; nor is it aggressive or threatening. It is more likely to be exercised by presenting choices, by opening or shutting off opportunities, than by coercive actions. One of the most obvious examples concerns how the existence of data-processing centres in the United States presented a choice to the European Union. The EU wanted data-driven companies to power its digital economy, and so it had to make choices regarding data-profiling rules and the free transfer of data to the US. The EU could ban the transmission and storage of EU citizens' personal data to the US but, if it did so, then it might compromise the ability of EU citizens to access services that have become essential. Of course, those firms lobbied to defend their power, and increased their activity when confronted with a decision-maker whose beliefs and values suggested a different course of action.

There is a duality about structural power – access or denial, empowerment or disempowerment, enabling or obstructing – that provides a way in for investigating the motives of the corporate industries that hold such control over the Internet, or would like to control it. It allows us to see how they are able to exert influence in ways that sometimes fail to synchronize with what we expect as citizens. That duality leads us to reflect on the empowerment narrative of the early Internet and seems to create a counter-narrative. That counter-narrative centres on the restrictive impact of the many different technologies, such as data-profiling, personalized Internet, zero rating, web-blocking, 'like'-button tracking and so on, and the way they can be applied to exert power.

The ability to block and filter is clearly a source of structural power that arises in several of the political agendas discussed. It enabled the broadband providers to change the arrangements for content delivery, and they defended it by turning policymakers away from a net-neutrality mandate. Blocking and filtering capability also led to demands from external interests to remove access to specific content, namely, for copyright enforcement and parental controls, and thereby presented conflicting policy choices for policymakers. The traditional entertainment industries have global resources to pressure governments,[1] but their structural power is deeply embedded in the offline world, and they were fighting to regain it in the online ecosystem. Hence, they targeted the Internet industries. When lobbying did not have the desired effect, they bypassed the political institutions and turned to the courts. Sometimes it backfired for the copyright holders, and entrenched the structural power of the new entrant, as it arguably did in the *Viacom* v. *YouTube* case.

The ability to offer preferred access is also a source of structural power that arose through both the net-neutrality and the data-profiling agendas. The industry wanted it in order to implement new pricing mechanisms such as zero rating, and so they sought to manoeuvre the law to legitimate this practice. What's less obvious is how preferred access can restrict the content available to the user. It does not matter whether it's done by a direct payment for faster transmission or through a bandwidth cap with zero-rated content. It would ultimately limit the choice available by simply ensuring it is too expensive for the user to access any other content.

Communications metadata from web-browsing and emails has become a source of power because the Internet industries have it and governments want it. States can only conduct surveillance of the Internet with the cooperation of the network providers, and the metadata becomes a bargaining chip. In exchange for assisting government with surveillance, the telecoms and Internet corporations gained an unquantifiable leverage over other areas of policy, and asked for liability protection. The way that the network providers wielded their structural power by demanding protection from liability is a recurring theme. Far from empowering individuals, this is a perilous world, and the perils for innovators are signalled in our final case. Cloud-service providers are about innovation, and also about new types of structures. They will shape the access to knowledge in a new way that we do not fully understand at the moment. They do not yet have the political power of the large content platforms and networks but, one day, they will do. The Megaupload case is a signal of what may happen to new structures which, maybe, just get a bit too big, and it also raises serious concerns about the rights of legitimate users of those services.

The following three examples attempt to capture some

of the possible combined effects of the different policies discussed in this book. What if Facebook is zero rated, incentivizing the user to choose Facebook over others, and, in addition, Facebook selectively presents content to the user's smartphone screen? In that scenario, the user's choice will be severely limited, yet under laws being brokered between governments and industry, it would be legal. Consider the same scenario with Twitter, which relies heavily on links. Twitter itself is zero-rated but reading the linked material is prohibitively expensive. As Twitter is widely used for political discussion, let us also suggest the scenario that a number of those links fall foul of filtering measures. All of this would also be legal, but restrictive. What about the innovator in the cloud, who is threatened with a blocking order if they don't allow interested parties (copyright holders or others) a backdoor to snoop on their clients' files? This too would be within the law. The network providers would be obligated to implement such an order as an exception to 'net neutrality', but the implementation would result in over-blocking of perfectly legitimate files, and the backdoor is an obvious privacy threat, likely to lead to self-censorship. These examples are not so far from reality in 2015. The extent to which they could be realized will depend on political choices.

The final task for this chapter is what to do about it? Should the power that shapes access to knowledge and shapes political agendas, itself be shaped for the benefit of society? There is a case for reformulating the regulatory problem in order to encapsulate that restrictive impact. Let's begin by considering the notion of the fingertap of desire that we discussed right at the beginning. This is a paraphrasing of the old Coca-Cola marketing maxim, meaning content is readily available on everyone's personal smartphone or computer, to quench their intellectual thirst, and all they have to do is tap their finger. The fingertap of desire invites an exploration of the multiple pressures on the tiny screen and the network that brings the content to it. The compilation of those pressures could, if allowed, create a restrictive effect which we might call the 'closing of the net'. Can this help us to take a new perspective on the regulatory equation?

Is there a case to impose public-interest duties on providers? If we argue that the corporations are in the position of providing public services, then the answer should be in the affirmative. It becomes a similar issue to regulating the water or power utilities. There's a reason why, when you turn on a tap, the water is clean, and why the gas company does not hesitate to fix a reported leak. They have to do it because they are operating a public service and if they don't they incur penalties imposed by the state.

The suggestion that the network operators are private companies that own their networks, and hence can have no public duties, is not supportable. Historically, all forms of public-communications services have been regulated in the public interest, and one can look back to the history of the telegraph and the telephone to see the basic principles. The precedent goes back to the railways.[2] The issue turns on protecting the rights of the public when using the service, as well as promoting fair competition on privately owned infrastructure. The Internet, with its technical complexity and worldwide reach, forces another look at these questions.

Human-rights principles suggest that states have a responsibility to ensure that private corporations do not violate the rights of citizens. Blanket measures addressed to society as a whole, to restrict free speech, are unacceptable. Proposals such as 'default-on' filtering would not comply. Any restriction on their activities online should be done within the scope of the law. It should only be carried out under the orders of a court, and not those of private corporations.[3] Restrictions should be narrowly scoped, and strictly necessary and proportionate to the issue they are intended to address, and implemented with judicial oversight.

The regulatory issues regarding the processing of personal data are about constraints placed on industry for the protection of privacy. Critical regulatory questions entail who should be allowed to get it and how it should be used. Additionally, who should oversee it and how do we make sure that the processes are in place to prevent abuses of power? There should be a rigorous assessment of the 'lawfulness, likely effectiveness and intrusiveness',[4] and policymakers should intervene in order to protect society from corrupt officials and politicians with malicious intent.[5] A regulator will need to have sufficient powers to address the possible abuses. Effective judicial and parliamentary oversight is required for surveillance.

Policymakers' calls for 'self-regulation' must then be called into question. This means the industry is expected to take responsibility for its own actions. However, industry is only likely to self-regulate in its own interest. Firms will only do so where they perceive a business benefit to themselves. Self-regulation rarely leads to a consideration of the public interest. Self-regulation also tends to ignore the harmful aspects of a technology,[6] because it is not in the industry's interest to consider them, and it will even try to cover up the harm, as, for example, with over-blocking.

Self-regulation arguably leaves the state exposed with regard to its duty to protect the fundamental rights to freedom of expression and privacy, both of which are threatened by content restrictions and surveillance measures. Of course, governments have to balance these rights against other rights that the state may have to protect. We have seen how, for example, the rhetoric of terrorism is drawn upon as a justification for greater privacy intrusion.

When two industries with conflicting interests are asked to self-regulate, it only entrenches the differences in their business models, and that is why 'cooperation' between the Internet service providers and the entertainment industry struggles to work without a court ruling. Self-regulation is also problematic where there is a clash of public interest, as in the British example of content-filtering, where the public interests in protecting children clashed with the public interest for an open Internet. When industry finds it is unable to legally protect its interests under self-regulation, it tends to run to the state seeking protection, as we saw in the content-filtering case.

For all these reasons, the whole notion of self-regulation is essentially promoted by states that seek to give a veneer of public acceptability to contentious measures.[7] The overall aim of policy should be to ensure that the long-term interests of all citizens are protected against short-term, commercial desires[8] or excessive state intrusion. Public accountability, incorporating judicial and administrative oversight, is recommended by the Council of Europe as part of the state's obligations under human-rights law. Disclosure obligations, overseen by a regulator with powers to audit, could be one realistic solution. Such obligations could include transparency measures, freedom-of-information laws and the possibility for judicial review.[9] The difficulty here would be to craft a law so that it imposes strict obligations on the large content platforms and network providers, but without harming small or medium-sized businesses.

Some corporations have defended their structural power by taking what they would call an ethical stance on certain difficult issues. For example, in defending themselves against allegations that they cooperated with the intelligence services, the large content platforms have publicized their own transparency reports and tried to distance themselves from the US government. They saw it in their own interest to curtail their assistance. Speaking to the *Financial Times*, Google's chairman Eric Schmidt said: 'The US made a huge mistake. It's naïve to think you can spy at this level and not be discovered [. . .] I was not responsible. I am opposed to it.'[10] One could observe that such ethical stances are dependent on the management, and when the management changes, the ethical stance may change too.

It is possible to use stronger forms of regulation. Industry can be forced to structure itself differently, in ways that are perceived as more beneficial from a public-interest perspective. This is indeed why Europe originally legislated for a competitive telecoms infrastructure.[11] Some experts[12] and academics[13] advocate vertical separation of Internet businesses, such that the network and content businesses would have to be kept separate, with regulatory oversight. Regulatory separation is an established concept in telecoms – it happens at a different level where the local network that brings the wires into homes is kept separate from the long-distance or trunk network – this is called functional separation. However, vertical separation is unlikely to happen in the near future. Market-oriented policymakers tend to prefer the opposite – vertical integration – where content and network are streamlined into one business, with the aim of generating enormous profits that can be reinvested.[14] This implies bundled services such as television over broadband and the so-called triple or quadruple play. It will be accepted by users for the convenience factor, in much the same way as they accept the Faustian pact of 'free' services in return for their data. The problem is that vertical integration ignores the structural-power issues and is more likely to exacerbate the restrictions on users.

Regulation is an appropriate response of the state to structural power, but it is not what private actors want. Therefore, political lobbying against regulation is the way that corporations seek to maintain or defend their structural power and that's why it's important to understand how they do this. Corporations seek to shape the political agenda in order to fend off regulation, or ring-fence it, and they do so in ways that are both indirect as well as direct. This book has shown examples of how they generally want either to ensure that a law in their favour is adopted, or to block a law that is not in their favour. They do this by obtaining, for example, the insertion or deletion of critical clauses in a proposed law, and there are several examples of methods that they will use in order to achieve this aim. Submitting ready-made amendments to parliamentarians is one method that is used, in the hope that such amendments will just slip through. This was what was observed during the processing of the 2009 Telecoms Package and also the Data Protection Regulation, although the volume of amendments – over 3,000 – was unusual and reflected the critical nature of data structures in the digital economy. It speaks volumes for the rapporteur, Jan Philipp Albrecht, that he did scrutinize them conscientiously and managed to broker a consensus.

Often, these amendments appear very simple – for example, a crossed-out phrase or sentence can be replaced with a new set of words that reflect the position of a different constituency of interest groups. Those small 'crossings-out' will extrapolate into major differences in the way individual people experience content, services and applications online. In the realpolitik of the Internet, the law can be changed to permit or prohibit with one stroke of the pen. Knowing how to make these changes is the stock-in-trade of lobbyists, and the skill is sometimes in making a subtle change which looks harmless to those who don't know the real agenda, but which can be loaded with interpretation. For example, the word 'cooperate' had a loaded meaning that was unknown outside of the immediate circle of interest groups in copyright-enforcement policy. Lobbyists also know that policymakers worry about sorting a 'compromise' that takes account of different stakeholders' positions, and will generally try to 'help' broker a deal that favours their organization. One tends to see this during tense negotiations, such as the EU trilogues over net neutrality and data protection, where there will be copies of the documents leaked and circulating, and feedback supplied to the rapporteurs.

Several of the cases in the book show how industry lobbyists embedded themselves in coalitions and entities with names that exude gravitas and public-interest concerns, such as the Future of Privacy Forum or the Creative and Media Business Alliance. From under these covers, they can run events and join committees without their sponsors or agendas being obvious. These are the aspects of industry lobbying that are the most devious and the most worrisome from a public-interest perspective. In very simple terms, a man who is paid by AT&T, or the Motion Picture Association, or BT, is unlikely to represent the interests of citizens. He is paid to ensure that government policies meet with what his corporation wants. If he achieves that, he is doing his job and his status will rise, as well as his pay packet. Thus, when one sees vendors of content-filtering systems on a ministerial committee for a policy that seeks to impose blocking measures, a red warning light should be triggered.

It's because we can see all the different cases together that we can recognize the interconnectedness of the policy decision-making. We can see how one decision impacts on another, and how different political initiatives – apparently isolated – are in fact linked. We can visualize the commercial and public-interest issues conjoined in the single image of the fingertap of desire. In doing so, it may help us to understand the impact of increasing restrictions as companies fight over the control of the user's access to content or do cooperative deals to obtain a preferential place within the user's allocation of 'free' bandwidth. The commercial incentive to get to the postcard-size screen is driving stock-market valuations. Conversely, the fingertap of desire means that the people who aren't in that preferential place will lose their voice. The 'open Internet' will still exist but it will be a luxury for those who can afford it, and the benefits of scale for small businesses and small media will be lost. Critically, there are many people nowadays who have little money but do have a smartphone or a laptop, and who rely on this technology to highlight political issues that otherwise would not be reported, so that without responsible regulation their views may be lost too. Thus, the potential risk of violating freedom of expression is significant and tangible, and with it comes the risk that democratic speech will be harmed. The imposition of restrictions therefore calls into question the state's duty to guarantee fundamental free-speech rights.

Internet restrictions will happen in different ways at different times. There is not a linear march of technology towards a restricted Internet. It is more likely to be a gradual closing, a piecemeal application of the barrier tape, not an abrupt dropping of the portcullis. It implies a growth of personalized, surveillance-based 'free' services, where the data may be shared with commercial partners and the government, resulting in an Internet that comprises a series of closed spaces instead of a single open network. The fingertap of desire signifies a narrowing of the prism in which we view and interact with knowledge, culture and beliefs. In that scenario, we must understand who controls access to that prism, and the political influence of the corporations that do so must be publicly accountable. The incentive to regulate in the public interest is clearly there; the question is whether governments will seize the opportunity to do so. It is important for all of society that the Internet stays open.

Notes

ACKNOWLEDGEMENTS

1 See the work of B. Guy Peters, and March and Olsen.

CHAPTER 1 POWER AND THE INTERNET

1 Source: International Telecommunications Union (ITU) statistics for 2015. Available at: <http://www.itu.int/>.
2 The book draws on the ideas of Susan Strange on structural power. See Strange (1988: 24–8).
3 Source: Statista.com at: <http://www.statista.com/statistics/371889/smartphone-worldwide-installed-base/>.
4 See the account in the official history of Coca-Cola on the company's own website, at: <http://www.coca-colacompany.com/history/the-world-belongs-to-the-discontented-coca-cola-forefather-robert-woodruffs-enduring-legacy>. More about Robert Woodruff can be seen in Wikipedia, at: <https://en.wikipedia.org/wiki/Robert_W._Woodruff>.
5 Bradshaw (2014).
6 See Cohen (2012) for a more theoretical discussion of this dichotomy. See also Mansell (2012), who suggests that the empowerment vision was not shared by policymakers.
7 Strange (1988: 24–8).
8 See also May (1996: 180, 185).
9 Ibid.: 187.
10 Strange (1988: 116–17).
11 Ibid.: 113, 120–1.
12 For the reader interested in this topic, Susan Strange even suggests the medieval Church as an example of a knowledge structure.
13 Source: International Telecommunications Union (ITU) statistics for 2015. Available at: <http://www.itu.int/>.

14 The application and presentation layers are also known as the service layer. Note that this explanation has been tailored for a non-technical reader. The layered model is known as the seven-layer model. The content sits on top of this model, and so it is not included. This is sometimes difficult for a non-technical reader to grasp. For the technical network experts, the content is something they do not deal with, hence it is outside the model.

15 This actually consists of the data link, network, transport and session layers, also referred to generically as the IP layer.

16 Belli (2013).

17 Crawford (2008).

18 The term is generally attributed to Tim Wu. See Wu (2003).

19 Wu (2003: 175, 142–3).

20 FCC Fact Sheet: Chairman Wheeler Proposes New Rules for Protecting the Open Internet, February 2015.

21 This definition is based on one drafted by the Dynamic Coalition on Network Neutrality, a group established under the auspices of the Internet Governance Forum (IGF), in a draft Network Neutrality Policy Statement, July 2015. Readers may also like to check Del Castillo 2014 Amendment 241, Catherine Trautmann, for the European Parliament's definition, which is similar. For an alternatively worded definition and comprehensive discussion of discrimination and net neutrality, see Van Schewick (2012).

22 Zuiderveen Borgesius (2015: 103–14); Pariser (2011).

23 See eMarketer, Worldwide Social Network Users: 2013 Forecast and Comparative Estimates. Available at: <http://www.emarketer.com>.

24 The Statistics Portal, leading social networks worldwide as of March 2015, ranked by number of active users (in millions); at: <http://www.statista.com/statistics/272014/global-social-networks-ranked-by-number-of-users/>.

25 Source: 'We are Social', a London-based social media consultancy.

26 EE (2015).

27 It is also an example of how Lawrence Lessig's 'code is law' theory applies. See Lessig (2006).

28 Strange (1988: 29, 45–50).

29 Zuiderveen Borgesius (2015).

30 Pariser (2011: 16).

31 See eMarketer, Worldwide Social Network Users: 2013 Forecast and Comparative Estimates. Available at: <http://www.emarketer.com>.

32 I am grateful for the input of Dr Didem Ozkul, Visiting Fellow at LSE, regarding the implications of location data.

33 Zuiderveen Borgesius (2015: 103–4).

34 I am grateful for the input of Jo Pierson, PhD, Associate Professor, iMinds-SMIT, Vrije Universiteit Brussel, regarding privacy and Facebook.

35 *Klass and Others* v. *Germany*, no 5029/71, §41; *Copland* v. *United Kingdom*, Application no. 62617/00; 3 April 2007, paragraph 41–2.

36 This idea is drawn from the earlier work of Frederik Zuiderveen Borgesius, University of Amsterdam; see also Pariser (2011).

37 Zuiderveen Borgesius (2015).

38 Strange (1988: 131).

39 Kaldor (1979: 65–8).

40 See Wu (2012) for an account of this historical trend.

41 Mansell (2012: 154–5).

42 Ibid.: 26.

43 Cohen (2012: 269–72).

44 See, for example, John Perry Barlow, Declaration of Independence of Cyberspace: 'Governments of the Industrial World, you weary giants of flesh and steel, I come from Cyberspace, the new home of Mind. On behalf of the future, I ask you of the past to leave us alone. You are not welcome among us. You have no sovereignty where we gather.' Published online at: <https://projects.eff.org/~barlow/Declaration-Final.html>.

45 For the US legal perspective, see discussion in Crawford (2008).

46 Under EU law, E-commerce Directive 2000/31/EC, Articles 12–15.

47 Mansell (2012: 14–20).

48 Conseil Consitutionel (2009).

49 Council of Europe Recommendation CM/Rec(2011)8 of the Committee of Ministers to member states on the protection and promotion of the universality, integrity and openness of the Internet.

50 EctHR Application no. 3111/10 *Yildirim* v. *Turkey*, Judgment, Final 18.03.2013.

51 European Convention on Human Rights. See: Council of Europe (1950), Article 10.

52 Scarlet Extended, EctHR Application no. 3111/10 *Yildirim* v. *Turkey*, Judgment, Final 18.03.2013, paragraph 69; Neij and *Sunde Kolmisoppi* v. *Sweden* no. 40397/12, Decision 19 February 2013, pp. 10–11; ECJ C-70/10, Scarlet Extended S.44–9; see also House of Lords, House of Commons 2010, on the Digital Economy Act.

Chapter 2 Private Lives, Public Policy

1 European Convention on Human Rights, Article 8.
2 Mansell (2012: 26–7, 154–5).
3 Strange (1988: 118).
4 See eMarketer, Worldwide Social Network Users: 2013 Forecast and Comparative Estimates. Available at: <http://www.emarketer.com>.
5 Pariser (2011: 16).
6 ICC (1992: 259).
7 This account has been prepared using ICC (1992).
8 Directive 95/46/EC of 24 October 1995 on the protection of individuals with regard to the processing of personal data and on the free movement of such data.
9 Heisenberg (2005: 1); Regan (1993: 264).
10 Kierkegaard (2005: 315); IAB (2001).
11 Directive 2002/2002/58/EC. concerning the processing of personal data and the protection of privacy in the electronic communications sector (directive on privacy and electronic communications). See also Kierkegaard (2005: 320); IAB (2001).
12 Internet Advertising Bureau UK. Full-year figures published for 2012, and 2014.
13 Internet Advertising Bureau press release: *EU Online Ad Market Surpasses €24.3bn in Value*, 23 May 2013. Available at: <http://www.iabuk.net/>.
14 European Commissioner for Justice, Viviane Reding, speech given at the 2nd Annual Cloud Computing Conference in Brussels, 7 March 2013: The EU's Data Protection Reform: Decision-Time is Now.
15 Zuiderveen Borgesius (2015: 103).
16 Zuiderveen Borgesius (2013: 83).
17 Ibid. See also Narayanan and Shmatikov (2008). Taking sample pseudonymized data from the NetFlix online television service, the authors of this paper were able to identify two individuals. They explain how, for example, ratings for a movie can reveal individual political preferences. They also explain how, even if identifiers such as names and social security numbers have been removed, the adversary can use background knowledge and cross-correlation with other databases to re-identify individual data records.
18 Future of Privacy Forum (2013b: 3): 'Specifically, pseudonymisation should excuse controllers from obligations

such as explicit consent, or rights of access and rectification.' Yahoo! (2013: 2–3); ICDP (2012).

19 Zuiderveen Borgesius (2013: 84). See also E-privacy Directive 2002/58/EC and 2009/136/EC.
20 Zuiderveen Borgesius (2013) contains a long discussion of this issue.
21 ICDP (2011). This is what is meant by 'streamlining and simplifying the EU's data transfer rules'.
22 TechAmerica Europe (2012); Digital Europe (2012a); ICDP (2011).
23 European Commission (2012).
24 See European Commission (2012) Recital 25 and Article 79 (6).
25 TechAmerica Europe (2012).
26 Ibid.
27 Digital Europe (2012a: 3).
28 Ibid.: 2.
29 TechAmerica Europe (2012).
30 He had been appointed to the role on 12 April 2012.
31 Author's interview with Jan Philipp Albrecht, June 2014.
32 Albrecht (2013a).
33 ICDP (2013a).
34 Digital Europe (2012a: 1). The phrase 'useless paper trails' was a reference to notions in the draft Data Protection Regulation on Privacy by Design and Privacy Impact Assessments, which could impose additional administrative overheads on to businesses.
35 Facebook (2013: 24): amendments to Recital 34 and Article 7(4).
36 Facebook (2013: 42).
37 Digital Europe (2013a: 2). For example, they wanted 'measures taken to ensure compliance with the Regulation' to be taken into account before sanctions would be applied.
38 The process of getting amendments tabled in this way is the stock-in-trade of lobbyists working in the European Parliament.
39 Author's interview with Jan Philipp Albrecht, June 2014.
40 ICDP (2011).
41 AmCham EU (2011).
42 ICDP (2012).
43 AmCham EU (2013: 8).
44 Coalition for Privacy and Free Trade (2013a).
45 AmCham EU (2013: 8).
46 Albrecht (2013a): Amendment 17: 'In order for processing to be lawful, personal data should be processed on the basis of the specific, informed and *explicit consent* of the person concerned

or some other legitimate basis, laid down by law, either in this Regulation or in other Union or Member State law as referred to in this Regulation.' (Italics added by author, to highlight the text commented on.)

47 Digital Europe (2012a: 2).

48 This information comes from a lobbying document circulated by the Dutch advocacy group known as Bits of Freedom, and seen by the author, entitled Amendments to the draft data-protection regulation, proposed by Bits of Freedom: Article 4(1).

49 Digital Europe (2013a: 3); Future of Privacy Forum (2013b: 3).

50 Albrecht (2013a) Amendment 100, 101, 102. Amendment 100, Article 6.1a (new): 'If none of the legal grounds for the processing of personal data referred to in paragraph 1 apply, processing of personal data shall be lawful if and to the extent that it is necessary for the purposes of the legitimate interests pursued by the controller, except where such interests are overridden by the interests or fundamental rights and freedoms of the data subject.' Amendment 101 sought to clarify the meaning of the legitimate interests of the data controller; Amendment 102 provided further guidance.

51 Future of Privacy Forum (2013a: 9).

52 Digital Europe (2013b).

53 United States International Trade Commission (2013).

54 In the European Parliament, consensus is the norm.

55 Albrecht (2013b).

56 Author's conversations with EDRi and Bits of Freedom.

57 ICDP (2013b).

58 Compromise 6 – Article 6.1 (f). Processing is necessary for the purposes of the legitimate interests pursued by the controller or, in case of disclosure, by the third party to whom the data is disclosed, and which meet the reasonable expectations of the data subject based on his or her relationship with the controller, except where such interests are overridden by the interests or fundamental rights and freedoms of the data subject which require protection of personal data. This shall not apply to processing carried out by public authorities in the performance of their tasks.

59 Compromise Article 20: Without prejudice to the provisions in Article 6 every natural person shall have the right to object profiling in accordance with Article 19. The data subject shall be informed about the right to object to profiling in a highly visible manner.

60 Data minimization (Compromise Article 5 (c)).
61 Compromise Article 40 and Recital 78: no transfers of EU
   citizens' data to third countries except where full compliance
   with EU law is guaranteed. Compromise Article 41: countries
   where Commission decides there is adequate level of protection
   (but this does not apply to the US) (Compromise Article 42: if a
   country does not have adequate protection or the organization
   does not ensure it, data may not be transferred).
62 Compromise Article 43a.
63 Fines up to €100,000,000 or 5 per cent of w/w turnover
   (Compromise Article 79(2a) c).
64 Author's interview with Jan Philipp Albrecht, June 2014.
65 Council of the European Union (2015b). This was the position at
   the time of going to press.

Chapter 3 The PRISM Agenda

1 William Kennard's speech was published on the website of the
  United States Mission to the EU (<http://useu.usmission.gov>)
  and headed 'Remarks by US Ambassador to the EU, William
  E. Kennard, at Forum Europe's 3rd Annual European Data
  Protection and Privacy Conference' (4 December 2012).
2 Fontanella-Khan and Chaffin (2013); Chaffin (2013).
3 Heisenberg (2005: 10).
4 Regan (1993: 264–5).
5 Directive 2002/58/EC on privacy and electronic communications.
6 Hengst (2013); Stratford and Johnston (2013). The German MEP
  Manfred Weber, from the Christian Socialist (CSU) Party, tried to
  terminate the 'safe harbor' agreement in 2014.
7 Heisenberg (2005: 74).
8 William Kennard's speech. See n.1 of this chapter, above.
9 Edward Snowden's revelations were published in the *Guardian*,
  the *Washington Post* and the German magazine *Der Spiegel*. Glenn
  Greenwald's book *No Place to Hide* (2014) has been used for this
  account.
10 Bowden (2013: 20).
11 Greenwald and MacAskill (2013); Greenwald (2013).
12 Bowden (2013: 28–9).
13 Greenwald (2013).
14 Ackerman (2013).
15 Gellman and Soltani (2013b).

16 Gellman and Soltani (2013a).
17 Curtis (2013).
18 Savage, Wyatt and Baker (2013).
19 Greenwald (2014: 151–60).
20 Ibid.: 136.
21 Savage, Wyatt and Baker (2013).
22 Clarke, R. A. et al. (2014: 14–20).
23 Savage, Wyatt and Baker (2013).
24 Ibid.; Clarke, R. A. et al. (2014: 21–5, 86–106).
25 Ibid.: 21.
26 Administration White Paper, Bulk Collection of Telephony
    Metadata, under Section 215 of the USA PATRIOT Act, 9 August
    2013, p. 17.
27 Clarke, R. A. et al. (2014: 36).
28 USA PATRIOT Act Uniting and Strengthening America by Providing
    Appropriate Tools Required to Intercept and Obstruct Terrorism (USA
    PATRIOT Act) Act of 2001: Public Law 107–56—Oct. 26, 2001. The full
    text can be found at H.R. 3162, GovTrack.us; see also Administration
    White Paper, Bulk Collection of Telephony Metadata, under Section
    215 of the USA PATRIOT Act, 9 August 2013, p. 1. For further
    information see Clarke, R. A. et al. (2014: 35, 48).
29 Hepting v. AT&T, no. C-06-0672-JCS Amended Complaint for
    Damages, Declaratory and Injunctive Relief, Demand for Jury
    Trial, 22 February 2006, pp. 6–8 (Available from the Electronic
    Frontier Foundation, which supported the action).
30 FISA Amendments Act (FAA) 2008, 50 USC 1801, Section 702.
31 Clarke, R. A. et al. (2014: 86–106); Bowden (2013: 22–4, 28–9).
32 FISA Amendments Act (FAA) 2008, 50 USC 1801, Section 802.
33 Clarke, R. A. et al. (2014: 95).
34 Greenwald (2014: 128–9).
35 Ackerman (2013).
36 See n.26 of this chapter, above: Administration White Paper,
    Bulk Collection of Telephony Metadata, p. 1.
37 Hujer and Schmitz (2013).
38 Letter from Viviane Reding, European Commissioner for Justice, to
    Eric Holder, US Attorney General, regarding PRISM, dated 10 June
    2013. A copy of the letter was circulated via the Statewatch website.
39 Nielsen (2013).
40 Hengst (2013).
41 Traynor (2013); Spiegel (2013).
42 Peel (2013).
43 Gathmann and Wittrock (2013); Appelbaum et al. (2013).

44 UK–US Communications Intelligence Agreement (UKUSA Agreement) dated 18 October 1956, released by the National Archives in the UK.

45 Goetz and Obermaier (2013).

46 Traynor (2013).

47 Weiland (2013).

48 Essers (2013); Weiland (2013); Peel (2013).

49 Amman et al. (2013).

50 Schmitz (2013a).

51 Schmid [the Echelon Report] (2001) and Campbell (2000).

52 European Parliament 2013 (Moraes Report) Clauses 31, 58, 59. The EU–US trade agreement referred to was TTIP (Transatlantic Trade and Investment Partnership), pp. 16 and 21.

53 Schmitz (2013b).

54 European Commission 2013a (Barroso statement TTIP).

55 Chaffin (2013).

56 Ibid.

57 Bowden (2013: 33).

58 Wolf (2013: 3).

59 Fontanella-Khan (2013a).

60 The author was told this by staff at the European Commission, DG Justice.

61 The inter-services draft of the General Data Protection Regulation was circulated by the website Statewatch and labelled Version 56 (29/11/2011).

62 Inter-services draft: see n.61 above. This text is taken from a copy of that draft, Article 42, as seen by the author.

63 Email dated 12 January 2012 released by the US Department of Commerce to the advocacy group Access Now under a Freedom of Information request. The email was sent by an official at the National Telecommunications and Information Administration, US Department of Commerce, to internal colleagues. It discusses a paper that is being drafted for the purpose of lobbying the European Union. Made available at <https://www.accessnow. org> on blog posting entitled *FOIA Documents Reveal Intensity of US Lobbying against the DPR*.

64 Digital Europe (2013a: 4–5).

65 Fontanella-Khan (2013b) plus supporting information from EDRi and AccessNow.

66 This account was prepared using emails released by the US Department of Commerce to the advocacy group Access Now under a Freedom of Information request and made available via

this webpage <https://www.accessnow.org/blog/2013/06/12/foia-documents-reveal-intensity-of-us-lobbying-against-the-dpr>. I also acknowledge the kind assistance of EDRi and Access Now.

67 Ibid. Access Now Freedom of Information request. The letter was one of the documents released.

68 See n.63 of this chapter, above.

69 Informal Note on Draft Data Protection Regulation (December 2011) made available online by European Digital Rights (EDRi) and seen by the author. See pp. 1 and 7–9.

70 The note was circulated by EDRi and seen by the author.

71 EDRi blog post by US lobbying against draft Data Protection Regulation. Available at: <https://edri.org/US-DPR/>.

72 Albrecht (2013a), Amendment 259, Article 43a: Transfers not authorized by Union law

> 1. Any judgments of a court or tribunal or any decision of an administrative authority of a third country requiring a controller or processor to transfer personal data shall only be recognised or be enforceable on the basis of, and in accordance with, a mutual assistance treaty or an international agreement in force between the requesting third country and the Union or a Member State.

73 Circulated by EDRi and seen by the author.

74 Strange (1988: 26).

CHAPTER 4 SURVEILLANCE LIABILITIES

1 Gamble (2003: para .4.0).

2 Deibert (2013: 45).

3 Bobbitt (2014).

4 Uncorrected transcripts of oral evidence to the Joint Committee on the Draft Communications Data Bill, Tuesday 10 July 2012 (Home Office), Q.10 Michael Ellis.

5 Uncorrected transcripts of oral evidence to the Joint Committee on the Draft Communications Data Bill, Wednesday 5 September 2012, Jimmy Wales and Nicolas Lansman.

6 Uncorrected transcripts of oral evidence to the Joint Committee on the Draft Communications Data Bill, Wednesday 5 September 2012, Malcolm Hutty.

7 German Internet exchange points as targets for surveillance, published by the consultancy BroadGroup at: <http://www.

datacentres.com/dc-news/german-internet-exchange-points-targets-surveillance>.

8 Uncorrected transcripts of oral evidence to the Joint Committee on the Draft Communications Data Bill, Tuesday 4 September 2012, Glyn Wintle.

9 50 USC § 1885a.

10 Bowden (2013: 20).

11 *Hepting* v. *AT&T*, US District Court (US District Court for the Northern District of California 3 June 2009). MDL Docket No 06-1791 VRW (Order) (Available from the Electronic Frontier Foundation which supported the action), p. 4.

12 *Hepting* v. *AT&T*, no. C-06-0672-JCS Amended complaint for damages, declaratory and injunctive relief, demand for jury trial, 22 February 2006 (Available from the Electronic Frontier Foundation which supported the action), p. 20. See also Declaration of Mark Klein, C-06-0672-VRW.

13 Ibid.

14 See n.11 of this chapter, above.

15 Public Law 114–23 114th Congress. The law was introduced to the House of Representatives as H.R. 2048.

16 See Clarke, R. A. et al. (2014); USA Freedom Act (H.R. 2048).

17 Paulson and Brigham (2015).

18 Joined Cases C-293/12 and C-594/12, Judgement of the Court (Grand Chamber) 8 April 2014 [Case C293/12 *Digital Rights Ireland Ltd* v. *The Minister for Communications, Marine and Natural Resources, the Minister for Justice, Equality and Law Reform, the Commissioner of the Garda Síochána Ireland and the Attorney General* (Request for a preliminary ruling from the High Court of Ireland); and Case C594/12 Kärntner Landesregierung, Michael Seitlinger and others: Request for a preliminary ruling from the Verfassungsgerichtshof (Austria).

19 Directive 2006/24/EC of the European Parliament and of the Council on the retention of data generated or processed in connection with the provision of publicly available electronic communications services or of public communications networks and amending Directive 2002/58/EC. Official Journal of the European Union L105/54 of 13 April 2006.

20 Council of the European Union (1998: 6–8).

21 The detail has been omitted from the main text: in August 2002, the Belgian presidency had drafted a text for what was called a Framework Decision on data retention. At the time, it is believed the Belgians sought the support of the British and

other governments; however, it was not pursued. In March 2004, after the Madrid bombings, both counter-terrorism and data-retention policies went up a gear. A 'Declaration on combating terrorism' on 25 March sought the establishment of 'rules on the retention of communications traffic data by service providers'. Shortly afterwards, on 29 April, the Framework Decision from 2002 was revised and a new draft was tabled. This new 2004 draft had the support of several member state governments, including notably the British, French, Irish and Swedish governments, but it didn't make much progress, and was rejected by the European Parliament on 7 June 2005. The 7 July London bombings were the catalyst for the ensuing events, when the whole process moved up into top gear. On 13 July, the Council prepared a Declaration, prioritizing an EU framework for counter-terrorism, with a specific brief for the British presidency.

22 Council of the European Union (2004).
23 Gamble (2002: para 2.3).
24 Ibid.: para 1.1.
25 Author's interviews with the Hertfordshire Constabulary, conducted in July 2006.
26 Email reply from Baroness Sarah Ludford to the author on 7 August 2006.
27 Sources in the Home Office and UK police interviewed by the author.
28 Council of the European Union (2005c).
29 Author's interviews with Michael Rotert, chairman of eco Verband der deutschen Internetwirtschaft e.V (the German Internet industry association), 9 July 2006; and Richard Nash, EuroISPA, 16 June 2006.
30 Justice and Home Affairs Council in Newcastle on 8–9 September 2005. Source: UK presidency of the EU website, Justice and Home Affairs Informal, Start date 8 September 2005. End date 9 September 2005. The website is no longer available; however, the author has a PDF of the page saved contemporaneously. The page reads: 'A plenary session on retention of telecommunications data followed, again chaired by the Home Secretary. Presentations on this issue were heard from police and industry representatives Jim Gamble (National Crime Squad); Professor Michael Rotert (European Internet Services Providers' Association) and Michael Bartholomew (European Telecommunications Network Operators' Association), and

concerned the benefits and costs of data retention. Discussion of this subject continued over lunch.'

31 Email reply from Baroness Ludford to the author on 7 August 2006.

32 Under the British presidency, the prime minister chairs when there is a meeting of heads of government, and individual ministers chair sub-meetings on their portfolios; in the Working Groups, the role of chair drops lower down the hierarchy to government officials.

33 European Parliament, debates 13 December 2005, Charles Clarke.

34 Ibid. See n.18 of this chapter, above, Joined Cases C-293/12 and C-594/12, Judgment of the Court (Grand Chamber), 8 April 2014 [Case C293/12 *Digital Rights Ireland Ltd* v. *Ireland*].

35 Presentation by expert Richard Clayton to ISPA Legal Forum on 9 March 2006, entitled *I Keep Six Honest Serving Men*, slide 3 (from contemporaneous notes taken by the author, who attended the presentation). Dr Clayton was referring to Article 5 of the directive, which sets out the types of data that the broadband providers have to retain. He said it was a 'technical nonsense'.

36 Breyer (2005: 365).

37 Council of the European Union (2005c: 6).

38 European Commission 2005. The difference was that a Framework Decision could be decided by the Council of Ministers alone, whereas a directive – under single-market policy – would be drafted by the Commission and be scrutinized by the Parliament. So this legalistic switch of instrument was significant, since it meant delays in the process, and the British presidency had to find a way round the problem.

39 One difference was that the stated aim of the Directive was to harmonize the requirements placed on network providers under the single market. This was done in order to comply with the single-market rules where laws governing the single market are usually made in order to harmonize some aspect of trade or service provision.

40 This account draws on Mr Alvaro's report (Alvaro 2005: 33–5).

41 Clarke (2005a). The British presidency appeared to take the view that storage and access should be considered as two separate issues, suggesting that since data was simply stored but not looked at, there was no issue with privacy protection.

42 Clarke (2005b).

43 There is a series of working notes where the presidency

communicates with the Council officials (who are known, in EU jargon, as COREPER). The notes state the Council viewpoint, and some also have a revised draft of either the Directive or the Framework Decision appended. Some are notes from COREPER to the presidency. They have been traced using their EU document numbers and references to previous or following documents. Reading through them, one can see how the presidency ensured that its amendments were made to the draft Directive. The documents are listed in the bibliography: see Council of the European Union (2005c–h).

44 Council of the European Union (2005d: 3).

45 Council of the European Union (2005e: 1–2, 5). An account of the trilogue discussion is on pp. 3–5.

46 Committee date obtained from European Parliament Procedure file.

47 Author's interview, 4 July 2006.

48 Ibid.

49 Ibid.

50 Criticism of Rapporteur Alvaro, Excerpts from the Greens/EFA Hearing 2005-12-07: Alexander ALVARO, ALDE. The text was made available by European Digital Rights (EDRi); however, the website where it was found by the author in 2006 is no longer available.

51 Author's interview, 4 July 2006.

52 European Parliament Debates, 13 December 2005, Ewa Klamt, EPP.

53 European Parliament Debates, 13 December 2005, Baroness Sarah Ludford, Sylvia-Yvonne Kaufmann and Kathalijne Buitenweg. The Left Group is officially GUE/NGL.

54 European Parliament, 13 December 2005, Sylvia-Yvonne Kaufmann.

55 European Parliament, Debates, 13 December 2005, Kathalijne Maria Buitenweg.

56 European Parliament debates, 13 December 2005, Sarah Ludford.

57 For example, Council of the European Union (2005d: 1).

58 Council of the European Union (2005f: 1).

59 Council of the European Union (2005g: 2).

60 Council of the European Union (2005h).

61 EDRi (2005).

62 Email from Baroness Sarah Ludford to the author in August 2006. NB: A proposal for a more limited data set was put to the Council meeting on 2 December but only the removal of one

item – the 'MAC address' – was accepted. The maximum storage time was set at twenty-four months (apparently this was a Council political manoeuvre at the request of Nicolas Sarkozy, the former French President, who in 2005 was the Interior Minister).

63 Baroness Sarah Ludford in email to the author, 7 August 2006.

64 Author's conversations with telecoms lobbyists in Brussels, in 2014.

65 The UK voluntary scheme operated under the Anti-terrorism Crime and Security Act 2001, part XI.

66 All Party Parliamentary Internet Group (2003), Recommendations 178 and 141. This report was not binding on the government, however.

67 Directive 2002/58/EC Electronic Privacy and Communications Directive.

68 Gamble (2002: S.1.2); APIG 2003 S.51–5; Council of Europe (1950).

69 Gamble (2002: S.2.1).

70 All Party Parliamentary Internet Group (2003) S.58–62; Gamble (2002: S.1.4 –1.5).

71 Gamble (2002: S.2.6).

72 Ibid.: S.4.2.

73 This kind of manoeuvre is known as 'policy laundering' – see Hosein (2004: 189).

74 See n.19 of this chapter, above, Joined Cases C-293/12 and C-594/12, Judgment of the Court (Grand Chamber), 8 April 2014 [Case C293/12 *Digital Rights Ireland Ltd* v. *Ireland*].

75 Council of Europe (1950).

76 Data Retention and Investigatory Powers Act 2014, Section 4 Extra-territoriality and Section 5 Meaning of a Telecommunications Service (8a).

77 Anderson (2015).

78 Internet Service Providers' Association (ISPA) Awards 2015 – David Anderson was named 'Internet hero'.

CHAPTER 5 NET NEUTRALITY UNDER PRESSURE

1 Summit on the Open Internet and Net Neutrality in Europe, 11 November 2010. The author attended. Quotes and description are from her own notes.

2 Quotes and examples are drawn from the author's notes of the meeting. Companies cited include Vodafone, Alcatel-Lucent, Deutsche Telecom and Cisco.

3 This definition is based on one drafted by the Dynamic Coalition on Network Neutrality, a group established under the auspices of the Internet Governance Forum (IGF), in a draft Network Neutrality Policy Statement, July 2015. Readers may also like to check Del Castillo (2014) Amendment 241, Catherine Trautmann, for the European Parliament's definition, which is similar. For an alternatively worded definition and comprehensive discussion of discrimination and net neutrality, see Van Schewick (2012).

4 See Council of Europe Declaration of the Committee of Ministers on network neutrality, 29 September 2010.

5 See Wu (2003).

6 Wu (2012: 59–60, 192–3).

7 The author used to write about the Baby Bells European investments, but has used Wikipedia as a fact check for the post-2005 developments.

8 Brown (2009).

9 Horten (2010) gives a detailed account of the net neutrality lobbying on the 2009 Telecoms Package and the correlation between the weakening of net neutrality and the cooperation agenda.

10 ETNO (2013: 1–2).

11 Ibid.: 2–4.

12 Ibid. See also Net Confidence Coalition (2009).

13 Responses to the European Commission Questionnaire on specific aspects of transparency, traffic management and switching in an Open Internet, October 2012 from BT (p. 9) and Telefonica (p. 9). BT (2012: 9); Telefonica (2012: 9).

14 Ibid. Vodafone's response, p. 16.

15 Microsoft advertising brochure from 2013.

16 This figure has been sourced from eMarketer, Worldwide Social Network Users: 2013 Forecast and Comparative Estimates, and The Statistics Portal, Leading social networks worldwide as of March 2015, ranked by number of active users (in millions). At: <http://www.statista.com/statistics/272014/global-social-networks-ranked-by-number-of-users/>.

17 Source: calculated using *Financial Times* equities data.

18 Source: Bradshaw (2014); and *Financial Times* equities data.

19 See n.13 of this chapter, above. BT (2012: 9).

20 Ibid.: 8, 10; see also Telefonica (2012: 6).

21 As described in ETNO (2012).

22 This is drawn from AT&T's submission to the 2012 European Commission consultation on the topic of net neutrality and the open Internet. It was headed: 'Comments of AT&T on the

European Commission's Public Consultation on Specific Aspects of Transparency, Traffic Management and Switching in an Open Internet. October 15, 2012', pp 13–15.

23 Author's interview with Pál Zarándy of consultancy Re-Wheel on 18 November 2014.

24 Letter from Ben Klass to Secretary General, Canadian Radio-television and Telecommunications Commission, dated 20 November 2013: Part 1 Application requesting fair treatment of Internet services by Bell Mobility, Inc., pursuant to CRTC 2010-445 and CRTC 2009-657, and the Telecommunications Act, s.24 & subsection 27(2).

25 Both European examples are from Digital Fuel Monitor, November 2014. Digital Fuel Monitor is a consultancy report produced by the Finnish telecoms consultancy, Re-Wheel.

26 The source was Jimmy Wales, speaking at the filming of Al Jazeera Head-to-head at the Oxford Union in November 2013.

27 See TTA (2012: 31, 73), and Appendix 7, p. 84. This is the Y2770 Deep-packet inspection technical standard submitted to the International Telecommunications Union (ITU) in 2012. It details at a technical level how deep-packet inspection functions on a network, and how it operates in conjunction with a content-filtering system.

28 This text and the account of a personalized network is taken from a promotional video released by the equipment vendor Procera Networks. At: <http://youtube/O7pbrFRJhic>.

29 Author's conversation with Erzsebet Fitori, Director, European Competitive Telecommunications Association (ECTA).

30 Telefonica (2012: 2, 5, 10).

31 Telefonica document from June 2015, seen by the author, commenting on a net-neutrality statement.

32 AT&T (2010: 183–7).

33 AT&T (2010: 188).

34 O'Brien (2009).

35 Net Confidence Coalition (2009).

36 Amendments circulated in Brussels in January 2009, and attributed to AT&T and the Net Confidence Coalition. As seen by the author. Horten (2010: 13) gives a detailed account of the net-neutrality lobbying on the 2009 Telecoms Package.

37 Author's discussion with telecoms lobbying consultant Caroline de Cock, in Brussels in 2011.

38 European Commission (2007b), Articles 20.5, 21.5, 22.3, and 21.6, and European Commission (2007a), Article 8.4g.

39 European Commission (2007c).
40 Horten (2010: 13); Horten (2012: 182). See Horten (2010) for a more detailed discussion.
41 A campaign by NGOs led by La Quadrature du Net, but including some from Spain, Germany, Italy and other member states.
42 Directive 2009/136/EC.
43 All three drafts were seen and analysed by the author.
44 European Commission (2013b). Its full title was 'Proposal for a Regulation of the European Parliament and of the Council laying down measures to complete the European single market for electronic communications and to achieve a Connected Continent'. Note that a regulation is imposed on all twenty-eight member states, who must implement it in exactly the same way, whereas a directive contains possibilities for member states to implement it in the way that suits them best.
45 European Commission (2013c).
46 This commentary draws on responses by BT, Vodafone and Telefonica to the European Commission consultation entitled *Questionnaire on Specific Aspects of Transparency, Traffic Management and Switching in an Open Internet* in 2012. All admit to the use of deep-packet inspection within their traffic-management systems.
47 BT's response to the European Commission's *Questionnaire on Specific Aspects of Transparency, Traffic Management and Switching in an Open Internet*. Submitted to the European Commission, 15 October 2012, pp. 8–10.
48 European Commission (2013b) Articles 21 and 23. See in particular: Article 23(2) End-users shall also be free to agree with either providers of electronic communications to the public or with providers of content, applications and services on the provision of specialized services with an enhanced quality of service. In order to enable the provision of specialized services to end-users, providers of content, applications and services and providers of electronic communications to the public shall be free to enter into agreements with each other to transmit the related data volumes or traffic as specialized services with a defined quality of service or dedicated capacity.
    Article 23(5) Within the limits of any contractually agreed data volumes or speeds for internet access services, providers of internet access services shall not restrict the freedoms provided for in paragraph 1 by blocking, slowing down, degrading or discriminating against specific content, applications or services,

or specific classes thereof, except in cases where it is necessary to apply reasonable traffic management measures. Reasonable traffic management measures shall be transparent, non-discriminatory, proportionate and necessary to [. . .] a/ implement a legislative provision or court order or impede serious crimes; . . . d/ minimize the effects of temporary or exceptional network congestion provided that equivalent types of traffic are treated equally.

49 BT's response to the European Commission's *Questionnaire on Specific Aspects of Transparency, Traffic Management and Switching in an Open Internet.* Submitted to the European Commission, 15 October 2012. See answers to Questions 17 and 18.

50 See Del Castillo (2014), amendments proposed by the Socialist and Liberal groups in the Parliament, April 2014.

51 European Parliament (2014), Article 21a, Amendments 234 and 241.

52 FCC (2010: 3).

53 Taylor (2014).

54 Ibid.

55 The White House (2014).

56 Crow (2014).

57 Letter from the FCC to AT&T's Senior Vice President – Federal Regulatory and Chief Privacy Officer, headed Re: Application of AT&T, Inc. ('AT&T' or the 'Company') and DIRECTV for Consent to Assign Licenses or Transfer Control of Licensees, MB Docket no. 14–90.

58 ETNO Press Release: Strengthening EU's digital economy: We need a positive conclusion to the 'Connected Continent' debate, 4 March 2015.

59 Council of the European Union (2015a).

60 Compare, for example, Council of the European Union (2014a: 5), point 11 and Council of the European Union (2014b: 25), Article 23.2; with Council of the European Union (2015c).

61 Van Bergen (2015).

62 Allen and Overy (2015).

63 Strange (1988: 28).

Chapter 6   Filtering Policy

1 Notes: UKCCIS Executive Board 9 September 2014, 15:00–16:00 Department for Education Chair: Edward Timpson, MP; Item 3, (<2014_09_09_UKCCIS_Executive_Board_Minutes2.pdf>).

2 See TTA (2012: 31, 73, and Appendix 7, p. 84). This is the Y2770 deep-packet inspection technical standard submitted to the International Telecommunications Union (ITU) in 2012. It details at a technical level how deep-packet inspection functions on a network, and it operates in conjunction with a content-filtering system.

In addition to consulting TTA (2012), this account of deep-packet inspection is drawn from product brochures of the manufacturers of deep-packet inspection equipment. They include Allot Communications and F5 Networks. Promotional videos from Procera Networks have also been viewed as part of this research. The author has seen live demonstrations of Procera systems at trade exhibitions.

3 E-commerce Directive 2000/31/EC Articles 12 and 15.

4 Directive 2000/31/EC of 8 June 2000 (the E-commerce Directive), Article 15.

5 Case number C-70/10 in the European Court of Justice, *Scarlet Extended* v. *Societe Belge des auteurs, compositeur, et editeurs* (*SABAM*), press release no 126/11, 24 November 2011.

6 Angelopoulos (2014: 3).

7 Ibid.: 4–5. It's also interesting to read the analysis by Judge Richard Arnold in the case *Cartier International* v. *British Sky Broadcasting*, starting at Section 158 (Principles to be applied). See n.18 of this chapter, below.

8 Case no: HC08C03346, *Twentieth Century Fox and others* v. *Newzbin Limited*, in the High Court of Justice, Chancery Division, 29 March 2010. See Kitchin (2010 S.135).

9 Directive 2009/140/EC, Article 1.3a. See Horten (2012).

10 Macdonald (2013a: 14).

11 Council of Europe (1950); and European Union (2001). This analysis draws on Angelopoulos (2014: 5).

12 House of Lords, House of Commons s.1.33: While striking a 'balance in the public interest' is an accurate description of the test for justification of infringement of the right to respect for possessions, justification of infringements of the right to freedom of expression and the right to respect for private life and correspondence require a different and more onerous exercise of justification by Government. The Government must show that the proposed interference is prescribed by law and necessary in a democratic society to meet a legitimate aim.

13 Zittrain (2008: 115).

14 European Court of Human Rights, Second Section, Case Of

Yildirim v. *Turkey* (Application no. 3111/10) Judgment Strasbourg, 18 December 2012, Final 18 March 2013, p. 29.

15 Although in a slightly different context, that of blocking a relatively limited list of webpages, and also domain seizure, Lord Macdonald's reports for the Internet Watch Foundation (p. 16, S3.9) and Nominet (p. 2) provide an interesting insight into the issue of private actors being asked to act as censors. See Madconald (2013a and b).

16 Department for Education (Bailey review) (2011), Recommendation 5.

17 See Livingstone (2014) and Livingstone, Haddon and Görzig (2012).

18 For example, a round table was held on 18 May 2011.

19 Author's conversation with Internet industry representative in 2014.

20 Case no. HC14C01382 in the High Court of Justice, *Cartier International* v. *British Sky Broadcasting*, 17 October 2014, Judgment.

21 Allot Communications and F5.

22 Final Notes from meeting of the UKCCIS Executive Board, 1 February 2012, 09:00–10:00, Home Office, London SW1 – see Item 4 (<UK-ccis.eb_notes_february_2012.pdf >).

23 UKCCIS Executive Board, 8 July 2013, Item 4, point 8; Item 2, points 5–6;) UKCCIS Executive Board, 9 September 2014, Item 5, points 23–7; and Ibid. footnote 41 UKCCIS Executive Board, 13 March 2014, points 7 & 8.

24 Final Notes from meeting of the UKCCIS Executive Board, 17 April 2012, 13:00–15:00, Department for Education, London SW1, Item 9, BlackBerry Filtering (<eb_notes_april_2012.pdf>).

25 Final Notes: UKCCIS Executive Board, 8 July 2013, 14.30–16.30, Department for Education, Item 5, International child Internet safety agenda, point 10. (<eb_notes_july_2013.pdf>).

26 Notes: UKCCIS Executive Board, 9 September 2014, 15:00–16:00, Department for Education, Chair: Edward Timpson, MP, Item 1 (<2014_09_09_UKCCIS_Executive_Board_Minutes2.pdf>).

27 UKCCIS Executive Board, 13 March 2014, 14:30–16:30, Home Office, Chair: Damian Green, MP, Item 2, Overblocking, point 3 (<Executive_Board_notes_March_2014.pdf>). See also UKCCIS Executive Board, 17 June 2014, 14:00–16:00, DCMS Chair: Ed Vaizey, MP, points 5–7 (<2014_07_10_UKCCIS_Executive_Board_Minutes_Final.pdf>).

28 FOSI website checked on 5 November 2014. FOSI is an industry
   association. The page headed 'Join FOSI' quoted membership
   fees for corporates and trade associations. <http://www.fosi.org/
   joining-fosi.html>. The list of members was obtained from page
   headed 'Membership', checked on 5 November 2014 and again on
   13 July 2015. At: <http://www.fosi.org/fosi-membership.html>.

29 The UK's Civil Service Code has strict rules for contacts between
   civil servants and lobbyists. Its principles were set out by the
   Nolan Committee in 1995. They include that 'holders of public
   office should take decisions solely in terms of the public interest.
   They should not do so in order to gain financial or other material
   benefits for themselves, their family, or their friends.'

   Here are selected extracts from *Guidance for Civil Servants:
   Contact With Lobbyists* published by the Cabinet Office:

   > These basic principles apply to all contacts between
   > civil servants and people outside Government, be they
   > businessmen, trades unionists, journalists or campaigners of
   > any kind.

   > Some things are completely unacceptable. For instance: do
   > not deliberately help a lobbyist to attract business by arranging
   > for clients to have privileged access to Ministers or undue
   > influence over policy. These would be serious disciplinary
   > offences and trigger procedures under which you would be
   > liable to dismissal.

   > Do not say or do anything that could be represented as granting
   > a lobbyist preferential or premature access to information,
   > parliamentary or governmental, which you have received
   > because of your official position.

   > Do consider whether meeting one group making
   > representations on a particular issue should be balanced
   > by offering other groups a similar opportunity to make
   > representations.

   > Do not give the impression to a lobbyist that any particular
   > advice, idea or information from their clients could or will
   > be decisive in the decision-making process. Decisions are for
   > Ministers who will want to weigh up all the evidence and all the
   > advice they receive before they judge the public interest.

30 Open Rights Group, at: <https://www.blocked.org.uk/isp-
   results>.

31 This was a tweet incorporating an image of Vodafone's intercept page, noticed by the author: @Claire Phipps My (work) phone when I click on the @guardian story about a proposed school for LGBT pupils *eyebrow*. At: <https://twitter.com/Claire_Phipps/status/556019324042104832>.

32 Vincent (2015).

33 Livingstone, Haddon and Görzig (2012).

34 Directive 2011/92/EU of 13 December 2011 on combating the sexual abuse and sexual exploitation of children and child pornography, and replacing Council Framework Decision 2004/68/JHA.

35 Source – author's conversations with Internet industry representatives.

36 The author is a Vodafone subscriber and has been through this process. Other sources include conversations with industry representatives.

37 Author's conversation with Internet industry representatives in 2014.

38 The reference is to Articles 12–15 of Directive 2000/31/EC, the E-commerce Directive. Many would argue that the mere conduit and 'no obligation to monitor' provisions should mean that the broadband providers could not filter on this wide-scale basis. The suggestion is that industry lawyers disagree.

39 Author's conversation with Internet industry representatives in 2013.

40 European Commission (2013b).

41 The leaked drafts were seen and analysed by the author. The same text appears in the final version.

42 European Commission (2013b) Recital 47.

43 Final notes: UKCCIS Executive Board, 8 July 2013, 14.30–16.30, Department for Education, Item 5, International child internet safety agenda (<eb_notes_july_2013.pdf>).

44 European Parliament (2014), Article 21a, Amendments 234 and 241.

45 Author's conversation with EDRi representative, June 2014.

46 Notes: UKCCIS Executive Board 9 September 2014, 15:00–16:00, Department for Education Chair: Edward Timpson, MP, Item 3 (<2014_09_09_UKCCIS_Executive_Board_Minutes2.pdf>).

47 Council of the European Union (2014b: 25, Article 23.2). The text reads: Except where specifically requested by an end-user,

providers of internet access services shall not apply traffic-management measures which block, slow down, alter, degrade or discriminate against specific content, applications or services, or specific classes thereof.
48 Council of the European Union (2015a: 5, Article 23.3(d)).
49 Council of the European Union (2015c).

CHAPTER 7 THE COOPERATION AGENDA

1 ISPs – Technical Options for Addressing Online Copyright Infringement – memo circulated by IFPI to Members of the European Parliament in 2007 and seen by the author.
2 See European Commission, Information Society and Media Directorate 2008 and associated stakeholder responses. This is also known as the Creative Content Online consultation of 2008. This entire account is drawn from submissions to this consultation from IFPI, MPA and CMBA.
3 Ibid.: IFPI submission, p. 14, to European Commission, Information Society and Media Directorate 2008.
4 Ibid.: submission from the CMBA, p. 7.
5 Ibid.: submission from the MPA, p. 9.
6 Horten (2012).
7 *Loi no. 2009–669 du 12 juin 2009 favorisant la diffusion et la protection de la création sur internet* (Legifrance 2009).
8 The figures come from the annual report published by Hadopi, a French government authority (title in French: *Hadopi Rapport d'Activite 2012–13*). Available at: <www.hadopi.fr>.
9 See n.3 of this chapter, above: European Commission, Information Society and Media Directorate 2008, submission from the CMBA, p. 9.
10 This quote is taken from an untitled submission to the European Commission consultation on the Review of the EU Regulatory Framework for electronic communications networks and services, from 27 October 2006. The submission is headed Creative and Media Business Alliance (CMBA), whose members included the Motion Picture Association (MPA) and the International Federation of Phonographic Industries (IFPI), as well as the Association of Commercial Television companies (ACT). See p. 4 of the document.
11 Ibid.; CBMA, from October 2006, p. 4.
12 One of the amendments addressed subscriber contracts in Article

20 of the Universal Services Directive, and the other was to insert copyright obligations into the Authorization Directive. See n.10 of this chapter, above; CBMA, from October 2006, p. 4.

13 European Commission (2007b). Universal Services Directive Article 20.6 and European Commission (2007a), Authorization Directive, Annexe 1, Point 19.

14 Horten (2012: 123). One clue is that the Impact Assessment European Commission (2007c) contained no reference to copyright – had these amendments been planned, the Impact Assessment would have had to discuss the issue of copyright.

15 Eurocinema letter: Eurocinema, Révision du Paquet telecoms 1 (28 April 2008). The letter was circulated in Brussels and made available on the Eurocinema website, hence seen by the author.

16 Analysis carried out by the author in 2008. This was Compromise CA3 to the Harbour report, as seen by the author in July 2008. The final version is Article 20.1 b in Directive 2009/136/EC.

17 Horten (2012: 139–51).

18 Ibid.; 148; Trautmann (2008). The full report included more than 800 amendments in several different documents. The amendment cited was Amendment 308. See also Harbour (2008). His report of 15 May 2008 incorporated 292 amendments accepted by the rapporteur.

19 Horten (2012: 145).

20 For the complete story of what happened to the copyright amendments in the 2009 EU Telecoms Package, see Horten (2012: 148–9).

21 Catherine Trautmann was on the Industry committee (abbreviated to ITRE) and was the lead rapporteur for the 2009 Telecoms Package. She was responsible for the Framework, Authorisation and Access Directives.

22 Horten (2012: 145–52). The final version is Article 33.3 in Directive 2009/136/EC.

23 European Parliament (2008a) Amendment 61, and European Parliament (2008b) Amendment 112.

24 Horten (2012: 198–204). See also the author's first-hand accounts on <www.iptegrity.com>.

25 See Angelopoulos (2014: 6).

26 Article 17.2 of the EU Charter of Fundamental Rights.

27 Article 10 of the European Convention on Human Rights or Article 11 of the Charter of Fundamental Rights.

28 The commitment took the form of a Declaration on Net

Neutrality drafted by the MEP Catherine Trautmann, and agreed on 4 November 2009. See also Horten (2012: 202).

29 See Directive 2009/136/EC, Article 20 and 21.

30 Eurocinema, *Lettre_depute_juillet08_final, Bruxelles 1 (Jul. 30, 2008)*, circulated in Brussels and on the Eurocinema website at the time, and seen by the author.

31 See MPAA (2010a: 4–17).

32 Letter from the MPAA to Ambassador Ron Kirk, United States Trade Representative, 22 November 2009, as seen by the author.

33 Ibid.

34 Horten (2013: 82–9).

35 See Cohen (2012: 2).

36 Case C-275/06 in the European Court of Justice, Productores de Música de España (Promusicae) v Telefónica de España SAU, Ruling of 29 January 2008.

37 Angelopoulos (2014).

38 See n.36 of this chapter, above. Case no. C-275/06 in the European Court of Justice, p. 1.

39 See Cohen (2012: 2).

CHAPTER 8 BLOCKING JUDGMENTS

1 Anthony White QC is quoted based on author's own notes at the hearing of *Twentieth Century Fox* v. *BT* at the High Court in London, June 2011, day 2.

2 I have chosen to focus on AT&T and Verizon as representative of North American telecoms companies, for the reason that they also conduct high-profile lobbying in the European Union.

3 Hannigan (2014).

4 Notes: UKCCIS Executive Board, 9 September 2014, 15:00–16:00. Department for Education Chair: Edward Timpson, MP Item 3 (<2014_09_09_UKCCIS_Executive_Board_Minutes2. pdf>); Item 4 Extremism, points 19 & 20.

5 The author is paraphrasing arguments put by representatives of some content platforms in 2014 at a meeting held under Chatham house rules.

6 For this interpretation, see Case no. 07 Civ. 2103 (LLS) *Viacom Inc* v. *YouTube Inc & Google Inc*, United States District Court Southern District of New York, Memorandum of Law in support of Defendants' motion for Summary Judgment, 11 March 2010. See also Case no. 07 Civ. 2103 (LLS) *Viacom Inc* v. *YouTube Inc &*

Google Inc, United States District Court Southern District of New York, Opinion and Order, 1 July 2008.

7 TorrentFreak (2013). Google Transparency Reports checked on 19 July 2015, and available at: <http://www.google.com/transparencyreport/removals/copyright/>.

8 Ibid.

9 Case no. C07-3783 JF *Stephanie Lenz* v. *Universal Music Corp (and Universal Publishing)* [2007] (20 August 2008).

10 Tom Frederikse, writing in Clintons Media News, emailed to the author on 2 October 2008.

11 EFF (2014).

12 Directive 2000/31/EC.

13 The author consulted on this point with legal experts including Innocenzo Genna and Andrez Guadamuz.

14 This was the proposed Notice and Action Directive – a draft of it was circulated among Brussels lobbyists, but it had not been pursued at the time of writing.

15 Case no. 07 Civ. 2103 (LLS) *Viacom Inc* v. *YouTube Inc & Google Inc*, United States District Court Southern District of New York, Opinion and Order, 1 July 2008.

16 Case no. 07 Civ. 2103 (LLS) *Viacom Inc* v. *YouTube Inc & Google Inc*, United States District Court Southern District of New York, Opinion, 23 June 2010.

17 Case no. 07 Civ. 2103 (LLS) *Viacom Inc* v. *YouTube Inc & Google Inc*, United States District Court Southern District of New York, Opinion, 4 April 2013. See Von Lohmann (2010). The case documents are available on the Electronic Frontier Foundation (EFF) website at: <https://www.eff.org/cases/viacom-v-youtube>.

18 BPI (2013).

19 BPI AGM 2012 – Geoff Taylor's speech, 5 July 2012, published by Record of the Day; at: <http://www.recordoftheday.com/news-and-press/bpi-agm-2012---geoff-taylor-speech>.

20 Case no. HC11C04518, *Dramatico Entertainment Ltd* v. *British Sky Broadcasting* in the High Court of Justice, Chancery Division, 20 February 2012, Judgment S. 26 –; Goldberg and Larsson, 2014.

21 Sunde (2012).

22 Stockholm District Court (2009: 54, 60).

23 Ibid.: 48.

24 Ibid.: 19–20.

25 Sunde (2012).

26 Letter seen by the author from John G. Malcolm, Executive Vice President and Director, Worldwide Anti-piracy, to the Honorable

Dan Eliasson, State Secretary, Ministry of Justice. It was dated 17 March 2006. Available at: <https://torrentfreak.com/images/pirate_mpa.pdf>.

27 2001/29/EC Article 8.3.

28 TorrentFreak (2008); IFPI (2008).

29 TorrentFreak (2012a).

30 For the full list to October 2014, see Case no. HC14C01382 in the High Court of Justice, *Cartier International* v. *British Sky Broadcasting*, 17 October 2014, Judgment S.52–6.

31 Directive 2001/29/EC (on copyright in the information society – it is referred to as the 'copyright' directive in telecoms industry, and the 'infosoc' directive in copyright policy).

32 Case no. HC08C03346, *Twentieth Century Fox and others* v. *Newzbin Limited*, in the High Court of Justice, Chancery Division, 29 March 2010. Kitchin (2010 S.135).

33 Case no. HC10C04385, *Twentieth Century Fox and others (The Members of the Motion Picture Association of America)* v. *BT*, in the High Court of Justice, Chancery Division, Respondent's Outline Submission, 23 June 2011. The author is relying on a printed version, handed to her in the court by a BT representative. The case is also sometimes referred to as the Newzbin2 case.

34 Ibid.: S.11–12.

35 Directive 2000/31/EC of 8 June 2000 (the E-commerce Directive) Article 15: specifies that no general obligation to monitor may be placed on ISPs by member states. In chapter 6 there is a longer discussion of the interpretation of this provision.

36 This was the Cleanfeed system, an automated system put in place to enable BT to meet specific requirements of the Internet Watch Foundation for the removal of child pornography, which is illegal in the UK. Case no. HC08C03346, *Twentieth Century Fox* v. *BT*. S.177.

37 Case no. HC08C03346 *Twentieth Century Fox* v. *BT*. S 186.

38 Case no. HC11C04518, *Dramatico Entertainment Ltd* v. *British Sky Broadcasting*, in the High Court of Justice, Chancery Division, 20 February 2012, Judgment.

39 Ibid., S.9.

40 Ibid., S.43 and S.71.

41 Ibid., S. 76–80.

42 Ibid., S.27 and S.28.

43 *Football Association Premier League* v. *BSkyB* (2013) S.56.

44 Cookson (2013); Torrent Freak (2013); Ghosh (2013).

45 Cookson (2013).

46 European Court of Human Rights, Second Section, Case Of
   Yildirim v. *Turkey* (Application no. 3111/10) Judgment Strasbourg,
   18 December 2012, Final 18/03/2013, p. 29.
47 Neij and Sunde Kolmisoppi against Sweden in the European
   court of Human Rights, Application no. 40397/12, 2013. This
   was an appeal made by two operators of The Pirate Bay to the
   European Court of Human Rights in 2013. In this instance, the
   court also upheld the decision of the Swedish court; however, it
   is interesting that it confirmed the engagement of the right to
   freedom of expression.
48 European Court of Human Rights, Second Section, Case of
   Yildirim v. *Turkey* (Application no. 3111/10) Judgment Strasbourg,
   18 December 2012, Final 18/03/2013, p. 29.

Chapter 9 A Dark Cloud

1 MPAA (2010a: 13–14; 2010b: 2).
2 MPAA members include Walt Disney, Paramount, Twentieth
  Century Fox, Sony Pictures, Universal and Warner Brothers.
3 Vinnell (2015) and 3News (2015).
4 Amsterdam and Rothken (2013: 18).
5 The raid was on 20 January New Zealand time, but appears to
  have been 19 January in the United States. The local date will
  be used throughout, as this will match up to document dates on
  other source material. Campbell (2012b).
6 Campbell (2012a).
7 Dvorak (2012).
8 EFF (2012).
9 MPAA (2010b: 5).
10 Ibid.
11 MPAA (2011).
12 DOJ (2010: 41, 47).
13 DOJ (2010: 14).
14 This account is drawn from information provided in a document
   known as the Carpathia warrant – this was the warrant to search
   the premises of Carpathia Hosting in relation to Ninja video:
   Case no. 1:10SW:32.0 in the United States District Court for the
   Eastern District of Virginia, Search & Seizure warrant 8 July
   2010. The warrant was made available as a PDF on the website of
   the magazine *Wired*, from where the author was able to download
   it. The PDF includes the 'Application For A Search Warrant' (p. 7

of the PDF), and the 'Application And Affidavit For A Search Warrant' (p. 8 of the PDF).

15 Ibid. Carpathia warrant. See 'Application And Affidavit For A Search Warrant' Section 8, p. 13 of PDF.

16 Ibid.

17 Ibid. Carpathia warrant, Affidavit, p. 9.

18 Ibid. Carpathia warrant, Attachment B, p. 26.

19 Amsterdam and Rothken (2013: 6).

20 Amsterdam and Rothken (2013: 27). Notice and take-down relates to United States law and the Digital Millennium Copyright Act (DMCA) which establishes a process for copyright owners to request that their content is removed from hosting sites and platforms, and a process for the platform and site owners to issue a counter-notice with their defence.

21 Mr Dotcom was speaking on New Zealand television. The interview was broadcast by 3 News, and was conducted by John Campbell on *Campbell Live* (Campbell 2012a).

22 Confirmation that it was the FBI, and the start date of the investigation, is cited in the warrant application to seize Megaupload's domain names: *Case 1:12-sw34 Document 145-1 in the United States District Court for the Eastern District of Virginia, Application for a warrant to seize property subject to forfeiture, 13 January 2013* (known as the Megaupload-domain seizure warrant).

Note there are four warrants and affidavits within one PDF that has been circulated. Three warrants are for domain name seizure, including megaupload.com. The fourth warrant is for search and seizure of the premises of Carpathia Hosting. The FBI investigation into Megaupload is confirmed in Case no 1:12-sw41 Affidavit in support of search warrant, where the warrant was requested to search the premises of Carpathia Hosting in Ashburn, Virginia, pp. 2–7 (these pages can be found on pp. 125–31 of the PDF).

23 Ibid. This account was prepared using information on pp. 126–31 of the PDF of the Megaupload-domain seizure warrant.

24 DOJ (2012b).

25 A superseding indictment was filed on 16 February 2012 and it is this document that is in the public domain and which is relied on here: *United States* v. *Kim Dotcom & others*: Criminal number 1:12 CR3, in the United States District Court For The Eastern District Of Virginia, *United States* v. *Kim Dotcom*

Megaupload Limited, Vestor Limited, Finn Batato, Julius Bencko, Sven Echternach, Mathias Ortmann, Andrus Nomm, and Bram Van Der Kol, Superseding Indictment, 16 February 2012, p. 1.
The Office of the US Attorneys, Criminal Resource Manual 655, Statute of Limitations and Defective Indictments, provides a definition of Superseding Indictments: If an indictment is dismissed because of legal defect or grand jury irregularity, the government may return a new indictment within six months of the date of dismissal or within the original limitation period (whichever is later).

26 Kim Dotcom interviewed 1 March 2012 by 3 News. At: <http://www.3news.co.nz/Kim-Dotcoms-first-TV-interview-Im-no-piracy-king/tabid/367/articleID/244830/Default.aspx>.

27 Vinnell (2015) and 3 News (2015).

28 Amsterdam and Rothken (2013).

29 Ibid.: 29.

30 Ibid.: 37.

31 Case no. CA526/2012[2013] NZCA 38. In the Court of Appeal of New Zealand between the United States of America and Kim Dotcom, judgment of the court, 1 March 2013, S.10.

32 Case no. CIV-2012-404-001928 [2013] NZHC 1269, High Court of New Zealand Auckland Registry. *Kim Dotcom & others* v. *Attorney-General*, In the matter of an application for judicial review and application for orders for interim relief pursuant to s 8, Judgment of Winkelmann J., 31 May 2013.

33 Campbell (2012b).

34 Ibid.

35 MPAA (2012).

36 Ibid.

37 See the following rulings. As this is an ongoing case, interested readers should check for up-to-date material in the New Zealand court archives.
Case no. CIV-2012-404-1928 [2012] NZHC 1494, High Court of New Zealand Auckland Registry. *Kim Dotcom & others* v. *Attorney-General*, Judgment of Winkelmann J., 28 June 2012.
Ibid. n.32 of this chapter, above: Case no. CIV-2012-404-001928 [2013] NZHC 1269, High Court of New Zealand Auckland Registry. *Kim Dotcom & others* v. *Attorney-General*, In the matter of an application for judicial review and application for orders for interim relief pursuant to s 8, Judgment of Winkelmann J., 31 May 2013.

CIV-2012-404-1928 [2014] NZHC 1505, High Court of New
Zealand Auckland Registry. *Kim Dotcom & others* v. *Attorney-
General*, In the matter of an application for judicial review and
application for interim relief pursuant to section 8, Judgment of
Winkelmann J., 2 July 2014.
See also Amsterdam and Rothken (2013: 7) for comment from
Megaupload's defence team. Her ruling was subsequently
overturned. The full records can be located in the archives of the
New Zealand courts.

38 See 3 News (2015); and Vinnell (2015). See also TorrentFreak
   (2014) and the court papers:
   Case no. SC30/2013 [2014] NZSC 24, in the Supreme Court of
   New Zealand, Between Kim Dotcom and others and The United
   States of America, Judgment of the court, 21 March 2014.
   Criminal no. 1:12 CR3, in the United States District Court for
   the Eastern District of Virginia, *United States* v. *Kim Dotcom
   and others*, Introduction and Summary of Evidence (undated
   document, released on 23 December 2013). It states: that the
   extradition hearing 'has recently been rescheduled to start on 7
   July 2014'.

39 Kidd (2015).

40 See also O'Neill (2014).

41 Farivar (2015) provides a detailed write-up of the civil forfeiture
   ruling in the US and New Zealand courts.

42 Weekes (2015).

43 Case no. 1:12-cr-00003LO *United States of America* v. *Kim Dotcom*,
   in the United States District Court for the Eastern District of
   Virginia, Brief of Interested Party Kyle Goodwin in Support of
   Emergency Motion for Protective Order by Non Party Carpathia
   Hosting, Inc. And For Additional Relief, 30 March 2012. The full
   case documents are available on the EFF website at: <https://
   www.eff.org/search/site/kyle%20goodwin?sort=created&order=d
   esc>.

44 Ibid.

45 TorrentFreak (2012b) and Amsterdam and Rothken (2013:
   38–41).

46 3News (2013).

47 Sandoval (2012).

48 See Gough (2008); McCullagh (2008); Cushing (2012).

49 McCullagh (2009).

50 This data is published by the Sunlight Foundation website,
   Motion Picture Association of America, Campaign finance,

available at: <http://influenceexplorer.com/organization/motion-picture-assn-of-america/90b570b10c2b4483a1af69149521324a#lobbying_section>.

51 Baker (2012).
52 This quote was widely reported. See Amsterdam and Rothken (2013: 2) and McCullagh (2012).
53 Motion Picture Association of America (MPAA) *Lobbying Reports* from the first quarter of 2009 through to the first quarter of 2012 were obtained and examined for this book. These reports disclose information as required under the US Lobbying Disclosure Act of 1995. The reports are available from the Clerk of the House of Representatives, Washington DC. In particular, see Motion Picture Association of America (MPAA) *Lobbying Reports* (2010 – Q2, Q3, Q4; 2011 – Q1, Q2, Q3, Q4).

CHAPTER 10 CLOSING PRESSURES

1 See Horten (2013).
2 See discussion in Wu (2003), and in Lee and Wu (2009). See also the work of Barbara Cherry on the common carriage principle. Other scholars of interest include Susan Crawford and Jack Balkin.
3 See Directive 2009/140/EC Article 1.3a.
4 Anderson (2015: 13(b)).
5 See also Clarke et al. (2014); *Klass and Others* v. *Germany*, no. 5029/71, §41; *Copland* v. *United Kingdom*, Application no. 62617/00, 3 April 2007, paragraph 41–2.
6 Morozov (2011: 282).
7 Cohen (2012: 269). For another discussion of self-regulation, see Zittrain and Palfrey (2008: 119).
8 Wu (2003).
9 I acknowledge the feedback of Francis Davey given during my presentation at the Gikii conference, Brighton, 2 September 2014.
10 Waters (2014).
11 See Michalis (2007) for a discussion of EU telecoms policy and competition.
12 Author's discussion with Pal Zarandy of Re-wheel/Digital Fuel Monitor, November 2014.
13 Wu (2012: 301–21).
14 Ibid.

References

The References are divided into a general bibliography, and a bibliography for EU and national government documents. The official document numbers are given for EU and government documents, where available. Official documents can usually be found online by typing the document number and title or keywords into a search engine.

GENERAL BIBLIOGRAPHY

3news (2013) Holder refutes Dotcom claims that US authorities were acting on behest of MPAA. In <http://www.3news.co.nz> 9 May 2013.

3News (2015) Kim Dotcom arrives in court for extradition hearing. Available <http://www.3news.co.nz> 21 September 2015.

Ackerman, S. (2013) Court order that allowed NSA surveillance is revealed for first time. In the *Guardian*, 19 November 2013. Available at: <www.guardian.com>.

Allen and Overy (2015) Net neutrality and the end of EU roaming charges – not there yet. Available at: <http://www.allenovery.com>.

All Party Parliamentary Internet Group (2003) *Communications Data: Report of an Inquiry by the All-Party Internet Group*, January 2003.

Amann et al. (2013) Germans rejected: US unlikely to offer 'no-spy' agreement. In *Der Spiegel*, 12 November 2013. Available at: <http://www.spiegel.de>.

AmCham EU (2011) *AmCham EU Hosts ICDP Inaugural Event with Vice-President Reding*. Press release dated 29 November 2011.

Amsterdam, R. R. and Rothken, I. P. (2013) *MegaUpload, the Copyright Lobby and the Future of Digital Rights: A White Paper*, May 2013. Available at: <http://robertamsterdam.com/the-kim-dotcom-megaupload-white-paper/>.

Anderson, D. (2015) *A Question of Trust: Report of the Investigatory Powers Review*. Available at: <www.gov.uk/government/publications>.

Angelopoulos, C. (2014) Are blocking injunctions against ISPs allowed in Europe? Copyright enforcement in the post-Telekabel EU legal landscape. In *Journal of Intellectual Property Law & Practice* 10(2014): 812–21.

APIG (2003) *All Party Parliamentary Internet Group: Communications Data: Report of an Inquiry by the All-Party Internet Group, January 2003*.

Appelbaum, J. et al. (2013) Merkel beschwert sich bei Obama. In *Spiegel Online*, 23 October 2013. Available at: <http://www.spiegel.de>.

AT&T (2010) *In the Matter of Preserving the Open Internet Broadband Industry Practices Comments of AT&T*, GN Docket no. 09-191 WC Docket no. 07-52, Before the Federal Communications Commission, Washington DC, 14 January 2010. Available at: <www.fcc.gov>.

Baker, Stewart (2012) The SOPA war: why the GOP turned on piracy (opinion). In the *Hollywood Reporter*, 2 February 2012. Available at: <www.hollywoodreporter.com>.

BBC News (2014) Pirate Bay fugitive Peter Sunde arrested in Sweden. In *BBC News Technology*, 2 June 2014. Available at: <www.bbc.co.uk>.

BCG (2013) *Reforming Europe's Telecoms Regulation to Enable the Digital Single Market*. Published by the European Telecommunications Network Operators' Association with the permission of the Boston Consulting Group, July 2013.

Belli, L (2013) *From 'End-to-End' to the 'Rule of Law': Should Network Neutrality Be Enshrined into Legislation?* Available at: <http://www.medialaws.eu/from-%E2%80%98end-to-end%E2%80%99-to-the-%E2%80%98rule-of-law%E2%80%99-should-network-neutrality-be-enshrined-into-legislation>.

Bits of Freedom (2013) Amendments to the draft data-protection regulation, proposed by Bits of Freedom. Available at: <https://www.bof.nl>.

Bobbitt, P. (2014) Tech companies have no right to define due process on data. In the *Financial Times*, 4 November 2014. Available at: <www.ft.com>.

Bowden, C. (2013) *The US Surveillance Programmes and Their Impact on EU Citizens' Fundamental Rights*. Brussels: European Parliament.

BPI (2013) *BPI Sends 50 Millionth Request to Google to Remove Illegal Content*. Press release, 15 November 2013.

Bradshaw, T. (2014) Facebook market value tops $200m. In the *Financial Times*, 9 September 2014. Available at: <www.ft.com>.

Breyer, Patrick (2005) Telecommunications data retention and human rights: the compatibility of blanket data retention with the ECHR. In *European Law Journal* 11/3: 365–75.

Bridy, A-M. (2012) Graduated response American style: 'six strikes' measured against five norms. In *Fordham Intellectual Property, Media and Entertainment Law Journal* 23/1 (2012): 2–66.

Brown, G. (2009) The internet is as vital as water and gas. In *The Times*, 16 June 2009. Available at: <www.thetimes.co.uk >.

Campbell, D. (2000) *Inside Echelon*. Available at: <www.Heise.de>, 25 July 2000.

Campbell, J. (2012a) Kim Dotcom's first TV interview: 'I'm no piracy king', transcript of broadcast interview on <www.3news.co.nz>, 1 March 2012.

Campbell, J. (2012b) Video: what really happened in the Dotcom raid. In 3News, 8 August. Available at: <www.3news.co.nz>.

Chaffin, J. (2013) Snooping claims add new complication to tough EU–US trade talks. In the *Financial Times*, 30 June 2013. Available at: <www.ft.com>.

Clarke, C. (2005a) Letter to Jean-Marie Cavada, Chairman LIBE Committee European Parliament. London: Home Office, 17 October 2005.

Clarke, C. (2005b) Government still pursuing agreement by Charles Clarke MP. Letter to the *Financial Times*, 7 November 2005. Available at: <www.ft.com>.

Clarke, R. A. et al. (2014) *The NSA Report, Liberty and Security in a Changing World*, Princeton: The President's Review Group on Intelligence and Communications Technologies, Princeton, NJ: Princeton University Press.

Coalition for Privacy and Free Trade (2013a) Comments of the Coalition for Privacy and Free Trade to the Trade Policy Staff Committee of the United States Trade Representative, Docket no. USTR-2013-0019, 9 May 2013. Available at: <http://privacyandtrade.org>.

Cohen, J. E. (2012) *Configuring the Networked Self – Law, Code and the Play of Everyday Practice*, New Haven, CT: Yale University Press.

Cookson, R. (2013) Anti-piracy drive sees Premier League mistakenly block websites. In the *Financial Times*, 15 August 2013. Available at: <www.ft.com>.

Coudert, F. and Werkers, E. (2008) In the aftermath of the Promusicae case: how to strike the right balance? In *International Journal of Law and Information Technology* 18: 50–71.

Crawford, Susan P, (2008) Transporting communications. In *Boston University Law Review* 89/3(2009): 871–937. Version cited is available at: <http://cgi2.www.law.umich.edu/_FacultyBioPage/faculty biopagenew.asp?ID=373>.

Crow, D. (2014) AT&T suspends superfast broadband plans. In the *Financial Times*, 12 November 2014. Available at: <www.ft.com>.

Curtis, S. (2013) Privacy International threatens telcos with legal action over Tempora. In the *Daily Telegraph*, 9 August 2013. Available at: <www.telegraph.co.uk>.

Cushing, T. (2012) Biden takes part in MPAA board meeting; suggests studios tell paying customers they're thieves. In *Techdirt*, 5 November 2012. Available at: <https://www.techdirt.com/>.

Deibert, R. (2013) *Shutting the Back Door: The Perils of National Security and Digital Surveillance Programmes*, Canadian Defence & Foreign Affairs Institute, Strategic Studies Working Group Papers. Available at: <http://cdfai.org>.

Deibert, R. et al. (2008) *Access Denied: The Practice and Policy of Global Internet Filtering*, Boston, MA: MIT Press.

Digital Europe (2012a) *Digital Europe Comments On Proposed European Commission's Regulation On Data Protection*, 12 March 2012. Available at: <http://www.digitaleurope.org>.

Digital Europe (2012b) *Draft Digital Europe Amendments*, 1 November 2012. Available at: <http://www.digitaleurope.org>.

Digital Europe (2013a) *Digital Europe Reaction to the Albrecht Report*, 25 February 2013. Available at: <http://www.digitaleurope.org>.

Digital Europe (2013b) *Digital Europe Comments on the Risk-based Approach*, 28 August 2013. Available at: <http://www.digitaleurope. org>.

DoJ (2010) *Joint Strategic Plan on Intellectual Property Enforcement*, US Intellectual Property Enforcement Coordinator, June 2010. Available at: <http://www.justice.gov>.

DoJ (2012a) *Leader Of NinjaVideo.net Website Sentenced To 22 Months In Prison For Criminal Copyright Conspiracy*. Press release issued by United States Department of Justice: United States Attorney's Office, 6 January 2012. Available at: <http://www.justice.gov>.

DoJ (2012b) *Justice Department Charges Leaders of Megaupload with Widespread Online Copyright Infringement*. Press release issued by United States Department of Justice: Office of Public Affairs, 19 January 2012. Available at: <http://www.justice.gov>.

Dvorak, J. (2012) Megaupload-equals-mega-fail-for-cloud-computing. In *PC Magazine*, 30 January 2012. Available at: <www.pcmag.com>.

EDRi (2005) *European Parliament Adopts the Directive on Data Retention*. Available at: <http://edri.org>.

EDRi (2013) *ENDitorial: Leaked Telecoms Regulation with or without Net Neutrality?* 17 July 2013. Available at: <http://edri.org/edrigram-number11-14telecom-regulation-net-neutrality/>.

EE (2015) *EE Announces World's Biggest Festival Phone Charging Service for Glastonbury 2015*. Press release, 20 May 2015.

EFF (2012) *Megaupload and the Government's Attack on Cloud Computing*, 31 October 2012. Available at: <https://www.eff.org>.

EFF (2014) *Lawrence Lessig Settles Fair Use Lawsuit over Phoenix Music Snippets*. Published online by the Electronic Frontier Foundation, 27 February 2014. Available at: <https://www.eff.org>.

Essers, L. (2013) US and Germany to enter no-spying agreement, German government says. In *Deutsche Welle* 14 August 2013. Available at: <www.dw.de.>.

ETNO (2012) *ETNO Paper on Contribution to WCIT: ITRs Proposal to Address New Internet Ecosystem*, September 2012. Available at: <http://www.etno.be/>.

ETNO (2013) *ETNO Position on Completing the Telecoms Single Market*. ETNO press release, 19 November 2013. Available at: <www.etno.eu/>.

Euro-ISPA (2005a) *Data Retention EU E-communications Industry Regrets Today's EP Vote, Putting Europe's Competitiveness and Information Society at Stake*. Press release: ECTA, ETNO, EuroISPA, GSM-Europe, ECCA, 14 December 2005. Available at: <http://www.ectaportal.com/>.

Farivar, C. (2015) Kim Dotcom gets to keep his millions, cars, and jet skis, for now. In *Ars Technica*, 3 June 2015. Available at: <http://arstechnica.com>.

Federal Communications Commission (FCC) (2008) *In the Matters of Formal Complaint of Free Press and Public Knowledge Against Comcast Corporation for Secretly Degrading Peer-to-Peer Applications*, 1 August 2008. Available at: <www.fcc.gov>.

Federal Communications Commission (FCC) (2010) *In the Matter of Preserving the Open Internet, Broadband Industry Practices Report and Order*, 23 December 2010. Available at: <www.fcc.gov>.

Federal Communications Commission (FCC) (2015) *Fact Sheet: Chairman Wheeler Proposes New Rules for Protecting the Open Internet*. Available at: <www.fcc.gov>.

Fontanella-Khan, J. (2013a) Brussels fights US data privacy push. In the *Financial Times*, 10 February 2013. Available at: <www.ft.com>.

Fontanella-Khan, J. (2013b) Washington pushed EU to dilute data protection. In the *Financial Times*, 12 June 2013. Available at: <www.ft.com>.

Fontanella-Khan, J. (2013c) Victory for tech giants on EU data laws. In the *Financial Times*, 25 October 2013. Available at: <www.ft.com>.

Fontanella-Khan, J. and Chaffin, J. (2013) US spying revelations raise fears over European co-operation. In the *Financial Times*, 2 July 2013. Available at: <www.ft.com>.

Future of Privacy Forum (2013a) *White Paper: The Draft General Data Protection Regulation: Costs and Paradoxes of Explicit Consent*. Available at: <www.futureofprivacy.org/>.

Future of Privacy Forum (2013b) *White Paper: The Definition of Personal Data: Seeing the Complete Spectrum*. Available at: <www.futureofprivacy.org/>.

Gamble, J. (2002) *Evidence of Jim Gamble to the All Party Internet Group (APIG) – Submission On behalf of UK Law Enforcement, 9.12.2002.*

Gans, J. (2011) The Rise of Content Platforms. In *Harvard Business Review*, 13 October 2011. Available at: <https://hbr.org>.

Gathmann, F. and Wittrock, P. (2013) Möglicher Lauschangriff: Realitätsschock für die Kanzlerin. In *Spiegel Online*, 24 October 2013. Available at: <http://www.spiegel.de>.

Gellman, B. and Soltani, A. (2013a) NSA collects millions of email address books globally. In the *Washington Post*, 14 October 2013. Available at: <https://www.washingtonpost.com/>.

Gellman, B. and Soltani, A. (2013b) NSA tracking cellphone locations worldwide, Snowden documents show. In the *Washington Post*, 4 December 2013. Available at: <https://www.washingtonpost.com/>.

Ghosh, S. (2013) Rights-holders taking down legitimate sites in piracy crackdown. In *PC Pro*, 14 August 2013. Available at: <http://www.alphr.com>.

Goetz, J. and Obermaier, F. (2013) Snowden enthuellt Namen der spaehenden Telekomfirmen. In *Suddeutsche Zeitung*, 2 August 2013. Available at: <http://www.sueddeutsche.de>.

Goldberg, D. and Larsson, L. (2014) Pirate Bay co-founder Peter Sunde: 'In prison you become brain-dead'. In the *Guardian*, 5 November 2014. Available at: <www.guardian.com>.

Goldsmith, J. and Wu, T. (2006) *Who Controls the Internet – Illusions of a Borderless World*, Oxford: Oxford University Press.

Gough, P. (2008) Joe Biden has a strong anti-piracy record. In the *Hollywood Reporter*, 23 August 2008. Available at: <www.hollywoodreporter.com>.

Greenwald, G. (2013) NSA collecting phone records of millions of Verizon customers. In the *Guardian*, 6 June 2013. Available at: <www.guardian.com>.

Greenwald, G. (2014) *No Place to Hide: Edward Snowden, the NSA and the Surveillance State*, London: Penguin Books (Hamish Hamilton).

Greenwald, G. and MacAskill, E. (2013) NSA Prism program taps in to user data of Apple, Google and others. In the *Guardian*, 7 June 2013. Available at: <www.guardian.com>.

Handelsblatt (2009) Mobilfunker wollen Skype in Funknetzen verbieten. In *Handelsblatt*, 9 April 2009. Available at: <http://www.handelsblatt.com/>.

Hannigan, R. (2014) The web is a terrorist's command-and-control network of choice. In the *Financial Times*, 3 November 2014. Available at: <www.ft.com>.

Harding, L. (2014) *The Snowden Files – the Inside Story of the World's Most Wanted Man*, London: Guardian Faber Publishing. Available at: <www.guardian.com>.

Heisenberg, D. (2005) *Negotiating Privacy – the European Union, the United States and Personal Data Protection*, Boulder, CO: Lynne Reiner Publishers.

Hengst, B. (2013) CSU-Politiker will Safe-Harbor-Pakt mit Washington kündigen. In *Spiegel Online*, 29 October 2013. Available at: <http://www.spiegel.de>.

Hopkins, N. and Borger, J. (2013) Exclusive: NSA pays £100m in secret funding for GCHQ. In the *Guardian*, 1 August 2014. Available at: <www.guardian.com>.

Horten, M. (1994) Road works – is the world ready for an information superhighway? In *Computing*, 14 April 1994.

Horten, M. (2010) *Where Copyright Enforcement and Net Neutrality Collide – How the EU Telecoms Package Supports Two Corporate Political Agendas for the Internet*, PIJIP Research Paper no. 17, Washington, DC: American University Washington College of Law.

Horten, M. (2012) *The Copyright Enforcement Enigma – Internet Politics and the 'Telecoms Package'*, Basingstoke: Palgrave Macmillan.

Horten, M. (2013) *A Copyright Masquerade: How Corporate Lobbying Threatens Online Freedoms*, London: Zed Books.

Hosein, I. (2004) The sources of laws: policy dynamics in a digital and terrorized world. In *The Information Society* 20/3: 187–9.

Hujer, M. and Schmitz, G. P. (2013) A leader should be careful about drawing red lines. In *Spiegel Online*, 16 September 2013. Available at: <http://www.spiegel.de>.

IAB (2001) *Europe's Telecom Ministers Reject Opt-in Regime for Cookies.* Press release, 12 December 2001.

ICC (1992) The proposed EC Data Protection Directive, protection of personal data – an international business view – comments of the International Chamber of Commerce. In *Computer Law and Security Report 1992* (8 November–December): 259–63.

ICDP (2011) *ICT Industry Joins Forces on Data Protection in Europe.*

Press release, 28 November 2011. Available at: <http://www.digital-europe.org>.

ICDP (2012) *Reforming Europe's Privacy Framework – How to Find the Right Balance*. Press release, September 2012. Available at: <http://www.euroispa.org/>.

ICDP (2013a) *Industry Concerned over Negative Impact of Albrecht Draft Report*. Press release, Brussels, 9 January 2013. Available at: <http://www.digitaleurope.org>.

ICDP (2013b) *Industry Groups Call On Council, European Parliament To Achieve Workable Data Protection Regulation; Concerns Remain Following LIBE Committee Vote on Draft Text*. Press release, 21 October 2013. Available at: http://www.digitaleurope.org

IFPI (2008) *Danish Court Confirms Pirate Bay is Illegal and Orders Access to be Blocked by ISP*. Press release, London, 27 November 2008. Available at: <http://www.ifpi.org/>.

International Chamber of Commerce (1992) Protection of personal data: an international business view – comments of the International Chamber of Commerce. In *The Computer Law and Security Report* (November–December 1992): 259–63.

Kaldor, M. (1979) *The Disintegrating West*, London: Pelican Books.

Kidd, R (2015) Kim Dotcom sold shares to pay for defence. In the *New Zealand Herald*, 8 October 2015. Available at: <http://www.nzherald.co.nz>.

Kierkegaard, S. (2005) How the cookies (almost) crumbled: privacy and lobbyism. In *Computer Law & Security Report* 21/4: 310–22

La Quadrature du Net (2008) *The 'Telecoms Package': Out of the Shadows, into the Light*. Press release, 10 July 2008. Available at: <http://www.laquadrature.net/>.

Lee, R. and Wu, T. (2009) Subsidizing creativity through network design: zero-pricing and net neutrality. In *The Journal of Economic Perspectives* 23/3: 61–76.

Lessig, L. (2006) *Code Version 2.0*, New York: Basic Books.

Livingstone, S. (2014) EU Kids Online: findings, methods, recommendations (deliverable D1.6), London: EU Kids Online, LSE.

Livingstone, S., Haddon, L. and Görzig, A. (2012) *Children, Risk and Safety on the Internet: Research and Policy Challenges in Comparative Perspective*, Bristol: Policy Press.

McChesney, R. W. (2013) *Digital Disconnect*, New York: The New Press.

McCullagh, D. (2008) Joe Biden's pro-RIAA, pro-FBI tech voting record. In *CNET*, 23 August 2008. Available at: <www.cnet.com>.

McCullagh, D. (2012) *How Republican Opposition De-railed SOPA and Protect-IP*. In *CNET*, 1 February. Available at: <www.cnet.com>.

Macdonald, K. (2013a) *A Human Rights Audit of the Internet Watch Foundation*, London: Matrix Chambers.

Macdonald, K. (2013b) *Review of UK Registration Policy*, December 2013. Available at: <http://www.nominet.org.uk>.

Mansell, R. E. (2012) *Imagining the Internet – Communication, Innovation, Governance*, Oxford: Oxford University Press.

March, J. G. and Olsen, J. P. (1984) The new institutionalism: organizational factors in political life. In *American Political Science Review* 78/3: 738–49.

May, C. (1996) Strange fruit: Susan Strange's theory of structural power in the international political economy. In *Global Society* 10/2: 167–89.

Michalis, M. (2007) *Governing European Communications*, Lanham, MD: Lexington Books.

Morozov, E. (2011) *The Net Delusion: How Not to Liberate the World*, London: Allen Lane.

MPAA (2010a) In the Matter of Preserving the Open Internet Broadband Industry Practices GN. Docket No 09-191; WC Docket no 07-52, Reply Comments of the Motion Picture Association of America, Before the Federal Communications Commission, Washington DC, 26 April 2010. Available at: <www.fcc.gov>.

MPAA (2010b) [To] Kira Alvarez, Deputy Assistant USTR, Re: Request for public comment on the 2010 Special 301 Out of Cycle Review of Notorious Markets. Docket no. USTR-2010-0029, Letter, dated 5 November 2010. Available at: <http://www.mpaa.org/>.

MPAA (2011) [To] Stan McCoy, Assistant US Trade Representative, Re: Request for Public Comment on the 2011 Special 301 Out of Cycle Review of Notorious Markets. Docket no. USTR-2011-0012, Letter, dated 26 October 2011. Available at: <http://www.mpaa.org>.

Narayanan, A. and Shmatikov, V. (2008) Robust De-anonymization of Large Sparse Datasets, in 2008 IEEE Symposium on Security and Privacy, Oakland, California, 18–21 May 2008, *Proceedings*, pp. 111–25. California: IEEE Computer Society.

Net Confidence Coalition (2009) *Ensuring Network Stability and Consumer Confidence in Competitive Markets*. Available at: <http://www.gsma.com/gsmaeurope/positions-and-publications/ensuring-network-stability-and-consumer-confidence-in-competitive-markets/>.

Nielsen, N. (2013) Leading EU party wants to ditch EU–US data agreement. In *EUObserver*, 29 October 2013. Available at: <http://euobserver.com>.

O'Brien, K. J. (2009) US lobbyists angle for influence in Europe's net-neutrality debate. In the *International Herald Tribune*, 8 March 2009. Available at: <www.nytimes.com/>.

OECD (2007) Internet Traffic Prioritisation: An Overview. Working Party on Telecommunication and Information Services Policies, DSTI/ICCP/TISP(2006)4/FINAL.

Ofcom (2012) *Ofcom Response to the European Commission Public Consultation on Specific Aspects of Transparency, Traffic Management and Switching in an Open Internet*, October 2012. Available at: <www.ofcom.org.uk>.

Ofcom (2014) *Ofcom Report on Internet Safety Measures – Internet Service Providers: Network-level Filtering Measures*, July 2014. Available at: <www.ofcom.org.uk>.

O'Neill, R. (2014) Embattled Kim Dotcom faces jail at bail hearing. In *ZDNet*, 29 November 2014. Available at: <www.zdnet.com>.

Owen, P. (2013) Spy agency chiefs defend surveillance – as it happened. In the *Guardian*, 7 November 2013. Available at: <www.guardian.com>.

Pariser, E. (2011) *The Filter Bubble – What the Internet is Hiding from You*, London: Penguin Books.

Paulson, M. and Brigham, G. (2015) Wikimedia *v.* NSA: *Wikimedia Foundation files suit against NSA to challenge upstream mass surveillance in Wikimedia blog*, 10 March 2015. Available at: <https://blog.wikimedia.org/2015/03/10/wikimedia-v-nsa/>.

Peel, Q. (2013) Germany to seek no spying deal with US. In the *Financial Times*, 12 August 2013. Available at: <www.ft.com>.

Peters, B. G (2005) *Institutional Theory in Political Science: The New Institutionalism*, New York: Continuum.

Poitras, L., Rosenbach, M., Schmid, F. and Stark, H. (2013) NSA horcht EU-Vertretungen mit Wanzen aus. In *Der Spiegel*, 29 June 2013. Available at: <www.spiegel.de>.

Reding, V. and Heilmann, T. (2013) Kleinstaaterei im Datenschutz muss aufhören. In *Die Welt*, 16 October 2013. Available at: <www.welt.de>.

Regan, P. M. (1993) The globalization of privacy: implications of recent changes in Europe. In *American Journal of Economics and Sociology* 52/3 (July 1993): 257–74.

Sandoval, G. (2012) *MPAA: Kim Dotcom's Conspiracy Theories are Bunk.* In CNET News, 5 July 2012. Available at: <www.cnet.com>.

Savage, C., Wyatt, E. and Baker, P. (2013) US confirms that it gathers online data overseas. In the *New York Times*, 6 June 2013. Available at: <www.nytimes.com/>.

Schmid, G. [the Echelon Report] (2001) *European Parliament Report on the Existence of a Global System for the Interception of Private and Commercial Communications (ECHELON Interception System)* (2001/2098(INI)), 37083.

Schmitz, G. P. (2013a) Trotz Abhöraffäre: Merkel bremst beim Datenschutz in Europa. In *Spiegel Online*, 28 October 2013. Available at: <http://www.spiegel.de>.

Schmitz, G. P. (2013b) Transatlantic Free Trade: US pushes for deal despite NSA scandal. In *Spiegel Online*, 11 November 2013. Available at: <www.spiegel.de>.

Spiegel Online (2013) Bundesregierung kritisiert US-Spähaktion scharf. In *Spiegel Online*, 1 July 2013. Available at: <www.spiegel.de>.

Spiegel, P. (2013) Hollande demands halt to 'unacceptable' US spying. In the *Financial Times*, 1 July 2013. Available at: <www.ft.com>.

Strange, S. (1988) *States and Markets: An Introduction to International Political Economy*, London: Pinter Publishers Ltd.

Stratford, J. and Johnston, T. (2013) *In the Matter of State Surveillance, Advice.* Report commissioned by the All Party Parliamentary Group on Drones, 22 January 2013.

Sunde, P. (2012) *Peter's Plea, in Falkwinge & Co, Aftermath of the Pirate Bay Trial: Peter Sunde's plea – In His Own Words*, 24 September 2012. Available at: <http://falkvinge.net/2012/07/06/aftermath-of-the-pirate-bay-trial-peter-Sunde's-plea-In-His-Own-Words>.

Sunstein, C. R. (2007) *Republic.com 2.0 – Revenge of the Blogs*, Princeton, NJ: Princeton University Press.

Taylor, P. (2014) FCC loses 'net neutrality' court ruling to Verizon. In the *Financial Times*, 15 January 2014. Available at: <www.ft.com>.

TorrentFreak (2008) *Pirate Bay Censorship Case Not Over Yet.* TorrentFreak website, 10 December 2008. Available at: <https://torrentfreak.com/>.

TorrentFreak (2012a) *Supreme Court Rules Pirate Bay Must Stay Blocked.* TorrentFreak website, 27 May 2012. Available at:<https://torrentfreak.com/>.

TorrentFreak (2012b) *Kim Dotcom: Joe Biden ordered the MegaUpload Shutdown.* TorrentFreak website, 3 July 2012. Available at: <https://torrentfreak.com/>.

TorrentFreak (2013) *Google Discarded 21,000,000 Take-down Requests in 2013.* TorrentFreak website, 27 December 2013. Available at: <https://torrentfreak.com/>.

TorrentFreak (2014) *Kim Dotcom Extradition Hearing Delayed until 2015.* TorrentFreak website, 7 July 2014. Available at: <https://torrentfreak.com/>.

Traynor, I. (2013) NSA spying row: bugging friends is unacceptable, warn Germans. In the *Guardian*, 1 July 2013. Available at: <www. guardian.com>.

TTA (2012) NGN: Requirements for Deep-Packet Inspection in Next-Generation Networks, Telecommunications Technology Association Standard – 2012-1357.Y.2770.

UKUSA Agreement (1956) *UK–US Communications Intelligence Agreement (UKUSA Agreement)* [As informally agreed on 10 October 1956]. In National Archives, Department HW, Series 80, Piece 11.

United States International Trade Commission (2013) In the matter of Digital Trade in the US and Global Economies, Testimony of Christopher Wolf, Inv. no. 332-540, Washington DC, 28 February 2013.

Van Bergen, M (2015) Roaming and net neutrality in Europe, is the end really near? Available at: <https://legalict.com/general/roaming-and-net-neutrality-in-europe-is-the-end-really-near/>.

Van Schewick, B. (2012) *Network Neutrality and Quality of Service: What a Non-Discrimination Rule Should Look Like*, Centre for Internet & Society, Stanford Law School, 11 June 2012.

Vincent, J. (2015) One in five sites blocked by the UK's over-zealous 'pornography filters'. In the *Independent*, 2 July 2015. Available at: <www.independent.co.uk/>.

Vinnell, K (2015a) Judge considers another Dotcom hearing delay. In <http://www.3news.co.nz> 21 September 2015

VON Coalition Europe, (2009) *Leading Providers of Voice Solutions over the Internet Protest Against Blocking or Degrading of VoIP Applications over Mobile Networks, after T-Mobile Announcement*. Press release from the VON Coalition Europe, 3 April 2009. Available at: <www. voneurope.eu/>.

Von Lohmann, F. (2010) *Viacom Makes Its Case against Yesterday's YouTube*. Published online by the Electronic Frontier Foundation, 27 February 2014. Available at: <https://www.eff.org>.

Waters, R. (2014) Big Tech at Bay. In the *Financial Times*, 15 September 2014. Available at: <www.ft.com>.

Weekes, J (2015) Dotcom facing financial 'battle' despite delayed case. In the *New Zealand Herald*, 2 October 2015.

Weiland, S. (2013) No-spy pact backfires on Berlin. In *Spiegel Online*, 13 August 2013. Available at: <http://www.spiegel.de>.

White House, the (2014) *Net Neutrality: President Obama's Plan for a Free and Open Internet*, 12 November 2014. Available at: <http:// www.whitehouse.gov>.

White, M. and Watt, N. (2005) Blair clinches deal with offer of big rebate cut. In the *Guardian*, Saturday, 17 December 2005. Available at: <www.guardian.com>.

Wu, T. (2003) Network neutrality, broadband discrimination. In *Journal on Telecommunications and High Technology Law* (2003) 2: 141–79.

Wu, T. (2012) *The Master Switch – The Rise and Fall of Information Empires*, London: Atlantic Books.

Yahoo! (2013) *Yahoo! Rationale for Amendments to Draft Data Protection Regulation as Relate to Pseudonymous Data*; 8 April 2013. Available at: <http://www.centerfordigitaldemocracy.org>.

Yu, P. (2014) The strategic and discursive contributions of the Max Planck principles for intellectual property provisions in bilateral and regional agreements. In *Drake Law Review Discourse* 62 (March 2014): 20–33.

Ziedler, C. (2013) Ein Datenschutz für 28 Länder. In *Der Tagespiegel*, 18 October 2013. Available at: <http://www.tagesspiegel.de>.

Zittrain, J. (2008) *The Future of the Internet*, London: Penguin Books.

Zittrain, J. and Palfrey, J. (2008) Reluctant gatekeepers: corporate ethics on a filtered Internet. In Deibert et al. (2008), *Access Denied: The Practice and Policy of Global Internet Filtering*, Cambridge, Massachusetts: MIT Press, pp. 103–22.

Zuiderveen Borgesius, F. (2013) Behavioural targeting: a European legal perspective. In *IEEE Security & Privacy* 11/1: 82–5.

Zuiderveen Borgesius, F. (2015) Informed Consent: We Can Do Better to Defend Privacy. In *IEEE Security & Privacy* 13/2: 103–7.

EUROPEAN UNION AND NATIONAL GOVERNMENT DOCUMENTS

Albrecht, Jan Philipp (2013a) Draft Report on the proposal for a regulation of the European Parliament and of the Council on the protection of individual with regard to the processing of personal data and on the free movement of such data (General Data Protection Regulation) [PE501.927v04-00], 16 January 2013.

Albrecht, Jan Philipp (2013b) Texts adopted Wednesday, 12 March 2014 – Strasbourg Provisional edition Protection of individuals with regard to the processing of personal data and on the free movement of such data (General Data Protection Regulation) (P7_TA-PROV(2014)0212).

Alvaro, A. (2005) Report on the proposal for a directive of the European Parliament and of the Council on the retention of data processed in connection with the provision of public electronic communication services and amending directive 2002/58/EC (COM 2005(0438) – C0293/ 2005 – 2005/0182 (COD)). European Parliament Committee on Civil Liberties, Justice and Home Affairs (LIBE) (A6 -0365/2005FINAL), 24 November 2005.

Article 29 Data Protection Working Party (2006) Opinion 3 2006 on the Directive 2006/24/EC of the European Parliament and of the Council on the retention of data generated or processed in connection with the provision of publicly available electronic communications services or of public communications networks and amending Directive 2002/58/EC, 25 March 2006.

Conseil Constitutionel (2009) Decision no. 2009-580 de 10 Juin 2009: *Loi favorisant la diffusion et la protection de la création sur internet*, Available at: <http://www.conseil-constitutionnel.fr>.

Council of Europe (1950) Convention for the protection of human rights and fundamental freedoms, as amended by protocol no. 11 (Rome, 4 November 1950), Registry of the Court of Human Rights, September 2003.

Council of Europe (2009) 1st Council of Europe Conference of Ministers responsible for Media and New Communication Services: A New Notion of Media? (28 and 29 May 2009, Reykjavik, Iceland),

Council of the European Union (1998) Note from Austrian Presidency to Police Co-operation Working Party. Interception of Telecommunications, Draft Council Resolution in relation to new technologies, 10951/98 REV2, 3 December 1998.

Council of the European Union (2004) Draft Framework Decision on the retention of data processed and stored in connection with the provision of publicly available electronic communications services 8958/04.

Council of the European Union (2005a) From Incoming Presidency to Working Party on Co-operation on Criminal Matters, 10609/05, 29 June 2005.

Council of the European Union (2005b) Outcome of Proceedings of Working Party on Cooperation in Criminal Matters, 4 and 5 July 2005, 11510/05, 27 July 2005.

Council of the European Union (2005c) Outcome of Proceedings of COREPER on 5 October 2005. 12894/1/05 REV 1, 10 October 2005.

Council of the European Union (2005d) Note from Presidency to COREPER. Subject: Data Retention. 13789/05, 28 October 2005.

Council of the European Union (2005e) Note from Presidency to COREPER. Subject: Data Retention: Trilogue Discussions with the European Parliament, 14328/05, 16 November 2005.

Council of the European Union (2005f) Note from Presidency to Delegations. Subject: Data Retention. 14935/05, 24 November 2005.

Council of the European Union (2005g) Note from Presidency to COREPER/JHA COUNCIL. Subject: Data Retention. 15101/05, 29 November 2005.

Council of the European Union (2005h) Outcome of Proceedings of JHA Council on 2 December 2005. 15449/05, 6 December 2005.

Council of the European Union (2014a) 15541/14 Note from Presidency to Delegations, 14 November 2014.

Council of the European Union (2014b) 15541/14 ADD1 Addendum to the Note from Presidency to Delegations, 14 November 2014.

Council of the European Union (2015a) 5439/15 Note from Presidency to Delegations, 20 January 2015.

Council of the European Union (2015b) 9165/15 Note from Presidency to Council, 26 May 2015.

Council of the European Union (2015c) 10409/15 Note from Presidency to Delegations, 6 July 2015.

Del Castillo (2014) Report Pilar del Castillo Vera European Single Market for Electronic Communications, A7-0190/2014, 27 March 2014.

Department for Education (Bailey review (2011)) *Letting Children Be Children Report of an Independent Review of the Commercialisation and Sexualisation of Childhood*. Presented to Parliament by the Secretary of State for Education by Command of Her Majesty, June 2011.

European Commission (2005) Proposal for a directive of the European Parliament and of the Council on the retention of data processed in connection with the provision of public electronic communications services and emending Directive 2002/58/EC.(COM (2005) 0438 FINAL. EN.), 21 September 2005.

European Commission (2007a) Proposal for a Directive of the European Parliament and of the Council amending Directives 2002/21/EC on a common regulatory framework for electronic communications networks and services, 2002/19/EC on access to, and interconnection of, electronic communications networks and services, and 2002/20/EC on the authorisation of electronic communications networks and services (presented by the Commission), Brussels, 13 November 2007.

European Commission (2007b) Proposal for a Directive of the European Parliament and of the Council amending Directive 2002/22/EC on universal service and users' rights relating to electronic communications networks, Directive 2002/58/EC concerning the processing of personal data and the protection of privacy in the electronic communications sector and Regulation (EC) No 2006/2004 on consumer protection cooperation (presented by the Commission), Brussels, 13 November 2007.

European Commission (2007c) SEC (2007) 1472, 90–92 *Commission Staff Working Document, Impact Assessment*, Brussels, 13 November 2007.

European Commission, Information Society and Media Directorate (2008) Communication from the Commission to the European Parliament, the Council, the European Economic and Social Committee and the Committee of the Regions on Creative Content Online in the Single Market COM (2007) 836 FINAL (Creative Content Online consultation), 3 January 2008.

European Commission (2009) Agreement on EU Telecoms Reform paves way for stronger consumer rights, an open Internet, a single European telecoms market and high-speed Internet connections for all citizens, Memo/09/491, Brussels, 5 November 2009.

European Commission (2012) Proposal for a Regulation of the European Parliament and of the Council on the protection of individuals with regard to the processing of personal data and on the free movement of such data (General Data Protection Regulation) COM(2012)11 Final, Brussels, 25 January 2012.

European Commission (2013a) Statement by President Barroso on the Transatlantic Trade and Investment Partnership, Berlin, 3 July 2013.

European Commission (2013b) Proposal for a Regulation of the European Parliament and of the Council laying down measures to complete the European single market for electronic communications and to achieve a Connected Continent, COM(2013) 627/3, 10 September 2013.

European Commission (2013c) *Commission Proposes Major Step Forward for Telecoms Single Market*. Press release, 11 September 2013.

European Parliament (2005) Debate on data retention, 13 December 2005.

European Parliament (2008a) European Parliament legislative resolution of 24 September 2008 on the proposal for a directive of the European Parliament and of the Council amending Directive 2002/21/EC on a common regulatory framework for electronic communications networks and services, Directive 2002/19/EC on access to, and interconnection of, electronic communications networks and associated facilities, and Directive 2002/20/EC on the authorisation of electronic communications networks and services (Codecision procedure: first reading) Texts Adopted By Parliament, 24 September 2008.

European Parliament (2008b) European Parliament legislative resolution of 24 September 2008 on the proposal for a directive of the European Parliament and of the Council amending Directive 2002/22/EC on universal service and users' rights relating to electronic communications networks, Directive 2002/58/EC concerning the processing of personal data and the protection of privacy in the electronic communications sector and Regulation (EC) no. 2006/2004 on consumer protection cooperation Texts Adopted By Parliament, 24 September 2008.

European Parliament (2012) Legislative Proposal Procedure File: Personal data protection: processing and free movement of data (General Data Protection Regulation) Procedure reference 2012/0011(COD).

European Parliament (2013) Draft Report on the US NSA surveillance programme, surveillance bodies in various member states and their impact on EU citizens' fundamental rights and on transatlantic cooperation in Justice and Home Affairs (2013/2188(INI)), Committee on Civil Liberties, Justice and Home Affairs Rapporteur: Claude Moraes (Moraes Report).

European Parliament (2014) European single market for electronic communications: European Parliament legislative resolution of 3 April 2014 on the proposal for a regulation of the European Parliament and of the Council laying down measures concerning the European single market for electronic communications and to achieve a Connected Continent; (Ordinary legislative procedure: first reading) P7_TA(2014)0281.

European Union (2001) Charter of Fundamental Rights: Official Journal of the European Communities, 2000/C 364/01, Charter of Fundamental Rights of the European Union, C 364/1–22.

Harbour, M. (2008) Draft Report on the proposal for a directive of the European Parliament and of the Council amending Directive 2002/22/EC on universal service and users' rights relating to electronic communications networks, Directive 2002/58/EC concerning the processing of personal data and the protection of privacy in the electronic communications sector and Regulation (EC) No 2006/2004 on consumer protection cooperation, Brussels, 15 May 2008.

Harbour, M. (2009) Amendments by the Parliament to the Council Common Position; Recommendation for second reading A6-0257/2009 Malcolm Harbour Electronic communications networks, personal data and the protection of privacy 16497/1/2008 – C6-0068/2009 – 2007/0248(COD) Council common position – amending Act, 29 April 2009.

House of Lords, House of Commons (2010) Joint Committee on Human Rights, Legislative Scrutiny: Digital Economy Bill, Fifth Report of session 2009–10, 5 February 2010.

Legifrance (2009) *Loi no. 2009-669 du 12 juin 2009 favorisant la diffusion et la protection de la création sur internet.* Available at: <http://www.legifrance.gouv.fr/>.

Trautmann, C. (2008) Draft Report on the proposal for a directive of the European Parliament and of the Council amending Directive 2002/21/EC on a common regulatory framework for electronic communications networks and services, Directive 2002/19/EC on access to, and interconnection of, electronic communications networks and services, and Directive 2002/20/EC on the authorisation of electronic communications networks and services, Brussels, 30 May 2008.

Trautmann, C. (2009) Amendment 001-001 by the Committee on Industry, Research and Energy, Recommendation for second reading, Catherine Trautmann A6-0272/2009, Electronics communications networks and services, 29 April 2009.

Index